COVENTRY'S MOTORCYCLE HERITAGE

I0879966

COVENTRY'S MOTORCYCLE HERITAGE

DAMIEN KIMBERLEY

The History Press

This book and its findings was made possible through the very generous support and funding obtained from the British Motorcycle Charitable Trust (www.bmct.org.uk) and Coventry Transport Museum (www.transport-museum.com)

First published 2009

The History Press
The Mill, Brimscombe Port
Stroud, Gloucestershire, GL5 2QG
www.thehistorypress.co.uk

Reprinted 2010, 2015

© Damien Kimberley, 2009

The right of Damien Kimberley to be identified as the Author of this work has been asserted in accordance with the Copyrights, Designs and Patents Act 1988.

All rights reserved. No part of this book may be reprinted or reproduced or utilised in any form or by any electronic, mechanical or other means, now known or hereafter invented, including photocopying and recording, or in any information storage or retrieval system, without the permission in writing from the Publishers.

British Library Cataloguing in Publication Data.
A catalogue record for this book is available from the British Library.

ISBN 978 0 07509 5125 8

Typesetting and origination by The History Press

CONTENTS

ACKNOWLEDGEMENTS

In compiling this publication, I would like to thank the following organisations for their most generous help and support: the British Motorcycle Charitable Trust, Coventry Transport Museum, the Vintage Motor Cycle Club, Mortons Media, the Motor Cycle Industry Association, the Antelope Club, Coventry Local Studies Library, Coventry Record Office, the 1901 Census Online and Ordnance Survey.

In obtaining certain information and photographs, I would also like to extend my gratitude to Leon Tavinor and Bert Yates Jnr, Sara J. Robinson and Pat Davis, Ron Ravenhall, John Raven, David Hamilton (Norcros Plc), John Belt, Kate Button, Annice Collett (VMCC), and Jayne Skayman (Mortons Media), A. Barber, Dave McMahon, John Hodson and Ned Sparkes.

W.J. Green (moustache) with staff at one of the Olympia shows during the 1920s selling his Omega motorcycles. (Green family archive)

INTRODUCTION

The motorcycle industry in Coventry developed over a period of some eighty years. Its origins stemmed from the enormous success of the city's bicycle trade, combined with the emergence and development of the motor engine towards the latter phases of the nineteenth century. The inevitable marriage of the two created the beginnings of an industry that would push the city to the forefront of motor production in Great Britain, while quickly gaining international acclaim as an industrial centre of excellence.

After the demise of the textile and watch trades in Coventry, the city was to become the birthplace of bicycle production in Great Britain, beginning as far back as 1868 with the manufacture of velocipedes at Josiah Turner's Coventry Machinists Co. Over the following years the physical form of the bicycle steadily improved, and in 1885 J.K. Starley discovered the pinnacle in designs with the 'safety' bicycle, which, by and large, still exists today.

At its peak in the early 1890s, the bicycle industry in Coventry was enormous, with manufacturers producing a combined 300,000 units per year, the highest concentration of bicycle production in the world. In 1896, Rudge-Whitworth alone produced some 75,000 machines, while in the same year the Coventry Premier Cycle Co. was claiming to be the largest bicycle company in the world. Astonishingly, it has been reported that during this time, approximately 40,000 people were involved in the manufacture of bicycles in Coventry – some two thirds of the working population.

Many years prior to this, the German, Gottlieb Daimler (1834–1900) had been fundamental in the development of the internal combustion engine, alongside Dr Nicolaus Otto, the original

The original works of the Coventry Machinists Co. Ltd, where the first velocipedes were built from late 1868. (Coventry Transport Museum)

J.K. Starley (1855–1901) seated on his 'Rover' safety bicycle in 1885. (Coventry Transport Museum)

Henry (Harry) John Lawson (1852–1925), one of the founder members of British Motor Syndicate. (Coventry Transport Museum)

patentee of the four-stroke engine principle. By 1885, Daimler fitted a vertical single-cylinder petrol engine to the reinforced frame of a 'Boneshaker' type cycle, paving the way for many others to follow. Daimler would later become the first motor manufacturing marque to be established in Coventry through Henry J. Lawson at a time of fast transition in the city. Many of the smaller bicycle manufacturers were disappearing, and those who did survive were forced to compete with one another by experimenting with the engine, discovering ways to apply them to two-, three- and four-wheeled vehicles.

Suddenly, many engineers were forming their own businesses and began to build their own motorized transport. Like cycle and car companies, the motorcycle manufacturers ranged in size depending upon how much financial backing they received. Companies like Humber, Singer, Triumph, Swift, Rudge and Francis-Barnett, with their large purpose-built factories, all prospered from such support and ran for many years, although not always without difficulty. Triumph sold 500 motorcycles in 1906, and by 1909 this figure had rose to an astonishing 9,000. By 1925 the company occupied 500,000 sq.ft of floor space and employed over 3,000 people. Meanwhile small opportunist firms such as Aurora, Kingsway, Lancer and Wigan-Barlow struggled to make an impact, surviving only a couple of years. In 1911, Wartnaby & Draper began making motorcycles in a small makeshift unit, but by 1913 they had exhausted their own private investments and closed.

The people who were involved in Coventry's motor industry came from all over the UK and beyond. Many were born locally and had previously worked in the city's cycle and watch trades, yet in the early days of the motor industry there was an apparent skills shortage in Coventry in specialised mechanical engineering. At this time the offer of high wages and job opportunities began drawing people to the city from places like London, Birmingham, Wolverhampton, Manchester and Crewe. Many came from Ireland, Wales and Scotland, and some from other parts of the world; for example, the 1901 census shows that 46-year-old German Richard

Muller was living in Coventry and working as a 'Motor Fitter', and Americans Frank Keegan and Charles Gurney were employed as 'Mechanical Engineers', as was 70-year-old Frenchman, Charles Collombier.

The development of the motorcar and the motorcycle in the city ran side by side in many respects, although this new technology did not come cheap as the prices of these new 'novelties' meant that only the very wealthy could afford them. The early motorcycles however, although still relatively expensive, initially provided the general public with a far cheaper option to that of the early motorcar, becoming ever more economic over the coming years, especially with the continuation of credit options introduced previously by many firms through sales of bicycles.

Throughout Coventry's history, there were well in excess of 350 individual bicycle manufacturers who operated in the city, over 120 motorcycle manufacturers, and somewhere in the region of 140 motorcar manufacturers. In addition to this were countless other associated companies acting as a conveyor-belt of production throughout the city. Body-builders, motor engineers, sidecar makers, machine-tool producers, pneumatic tyre and chain manufacturers are just some examples, all benefiting from and assisting the Coventry motor industry to reach international success. The result was that all of these respected trades provided jobs and attracted people from all parts of the kingdom and from all walks of life to Coventry in a very short space of time. So much so that between 1891 and 1921, the population of Coventry had risen from 52,742 to 128,157 – an increase of more than 75,000 in just thirty years. The transport industry alone was the prime catalyst for this mass influx of people, all looking to improve their career prospects, and, in-turn, their quality of life.

This rapid growth forced the city to evolve and adapt its entire infrastructure, thus shaping much of the Coventry that exists today. During the Second World War many factories switched to the production of armaments in support of the national war effort, which meant that the city suddenly became a major target of the German Luftwaffe. The resulting air raids reduced much of the city to rubble, forcing town planners to once again redevelop large areas.

The motorcycle trade was a major force in the industrial and economic development of Coventry during the twentieth century until its final demise, at the hands of foreign competition, with the closure of Triumph Motorcycles Ltd in 1982.

In April 2006, Coventry Transport Museum unveiled a new Motorcycle Gallery, supported through the generosity and commitment of the British Motorcycle Charitable Trust (BMCT). The Museum now holds many fine examples of Coventry-manufactured motorcycles, from rare examples such as Omega and Revere, through to Coventry Eagles, Rudge's and Triumphs. Although the factories are now all gone, the proud legacy of Coventry-built motorcycles still remains in museums, archives and private collections around the world.

The great Rudge-Whitworth factory taken from Trafalgar Street in 1912. This picture was taken by the Lion Foundry to demonstrate the strength of their fitted fire escape. (Norcros Ltd)

Rudge-Whitworth's motorcycle testing shop in 1912. (Coventry Transport Museum)

A group of Coventry 'testers' at Stoneleigh Hill in 1906. (Coventry Transport Museum)

Rex Works 'testers' in 1908, with Richard Lord pictured second from the right. (Coventry Transport Museum)

Two women in Edwardian dress try out a ladies Rex model in Coventry. (Coventry Transport Museum)

Another Rex motorcycle, this time needing roadside attention during a Warwickshire outing. (Coventry Transport Museum)

Len Crisp competes on his Humber machine in 1926. (Coventry Transport Museum)

A–Z OF COVENTRY MOTORCYCLE MANUFACTURERS & MARQUES

The following is an alphabetical list of all known Coventry motorcycle manufacturers and marques to date. Many of the larger companies and their products have been well documented over the years, including the likes of Triumph, Rudge and Francis Barnett. Others, however, have been recently discovered through more thorough research, where in many cases the individuals behind the origins of the businesses had been forgotten. This list therefore hopes to provide, where possible, information surrounding the people who founded or worked for the companies.

The dates supplied are those in which the individual companies are thought to have produced motorcycles based on research compiled to date. The dates shown in brackets indicate the probable lifespan of the company working in other areas outside motorcycle production. This list also includes motorised tricycles, forecars and other near related vehicles.

If anyone has any new or further information, or photographs relevant to any of the following companies and individuals, then Coventry Transport Museum would be very interested to acquire such information so that we can update our records.

ACCLES, 1896–1898

H.J. Lawson, Motor Mills, Drapers Field

The Accles motorised bicycle and tricycle was built for Harry J. Lawson's British Motor Syndicate under the supervision of Charles McRobie-Turrell between 1896 and 1898. Based on the De Dion Bouton principle, it had been designed by two Australian brothers, James and William Accles, who were by this time living in England and working as 'Mechanical Engineers'. Lawson had recently purchased an ex-cotton factory in the Drapers Field area of Coventry, which he renamed the 'Motor Mills', a place where much early experimental and pioneering engineering work was to be carried out. Through his contacts he was informed of the Accles design and, after negotiations, had it brought to life at the factory, most probably built using the Humber workforce. In his 1955 book *Motor Cycles History & Development*, C.F. Caunter states,

The Accles motor-bicycle was just one of many projects that H.J. Lawson concerned himself with. (Vintage Motor Cycle Club)

'another Coventry product of the same year (1898) was the Accles tricycle, which was built for the newly formed British Motor Syndicate founded by H.J. Lawson; this machine was generally similar to the De Dion-Bouton design, particularly with regard to the engine'. The Accles brothers, along with Frederick H. De Veulle, were later involved with William A. Starley's motorcycle of 1903 in Coventry, a design that was later taken on by the Swift Motor Co.
(See also Humber, and Lawson.)

ACME, 1902–1920

Acme Motor Co. Ltd, Earlsdon Works, Osborne Road & 4 Lincoln Street, Earlsdon

The Acme Motor Co. Ltd was established at Earlsdon, Coventry in 1902, their name being chosen for its Latin meaning – 'the highest point of perfection or achievement'. Although not known for certain, the founder of this firm may well have been Frederick Allard, who in 1901 sold his cycle and motor business to the Birmingham Motor Manufacturing Co. Acme's first motor-bicycles were fitted with 2hp Minerva engines, auto motors, and later, engines of their own manufacture. Many motor advertising slogans of the era tended to exaggerate, often claiming that the motorcycles produced were capable of doing things they probably couldn't. Acme's slogan was no different, stating that their motorcycles were 'the machines of no regrets'. The company were keen to break into competition racing, and in 1908 they entered two Acme Twins in the Isle of Man TT, but unfortunately both failed to complete the course. By 1911, they added sidecars to their products alongside a steady stream of motorcycles of varying engine sizes. In 1920 the company changed its name to Coventry Acme, but just two years later merged with Earlsdon neighbours Rex to form Rex-Acme. They added the Hobart concern to drive the company forward in 1923, but for unknown reasons that failed to take off. This did not affect Rex-Acme too badly though and they continued to build motorcycles for a further ten years.
(See also Allard, Coventry Acme, Hobart-Acme, and Rex-Acme.)

An Acme JAP-powered motorcycle outfit of 1920. (Mortons Media)

AEC, 1914–1924

Auto Engineering Co. Ltd, Springfield Place, 590a Stoney Stanton Road

AEC owner Joseph William Wareing was born in Daventry, Northamptonshire in 1879. Having first worked in the cycle trade in his native town, in the early 1900s he moved to Coventry and became a 'Cycle Maker and General Machinist' at one of the city's many cycle manufacturers. After some twenty years in the industry he set up the Auto Engineering Co. in 1914 at modest works on Stoney Stanton Road. Although predominately a general engineering concern, AEC did experiment with motorcycle production on a limited scale, building a 211cc two-stroke powered model of basic design named the 'Motor-Cyclette'. Although the AEC was first produced at the outbreak of the First World War, it was still a cost-effective machine and sold relatively well, yet ultimately the competitive price-wars of the 1920s was too much to bear, Wareing's last motorcycle being sold in 1924.

Detail of the AEC power unit built by the Auto Engineering Co. (Vintage Motor Cycle Club)

AEL, 1919–1924

A.E. Lynes & Co. Ltd, 38 Moor Street, Earlsdon

Arthur Edward Lynes began this business at 38 Moor Street, Earlsdon in 1919, next door to the Earlsdon Motor Body & Carriage Works. His past activities however have been somewhat distorted over the years. As well as supplying motorcycles, some have reported that he was an engineer and cycle maker, others that he was a retail spares and accessories dealer. The confusion really lies in whether he built his own motorcycles or simply purchased other makes,

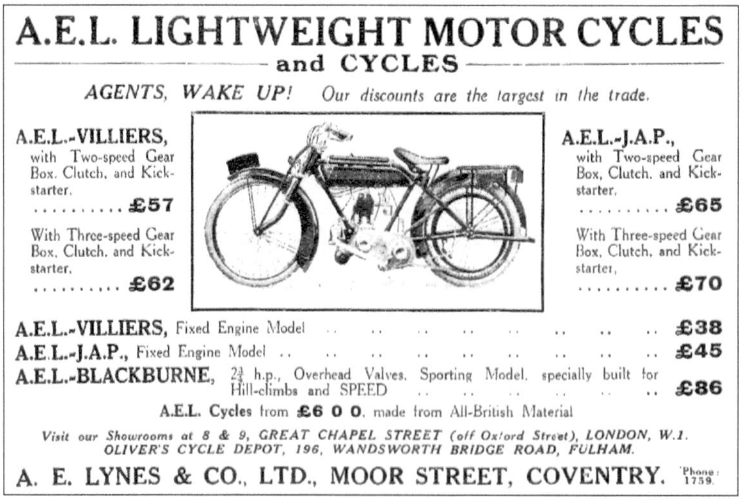

Arthur Lynes used various engines to power his AEL machines. (Vintage Motor Cycle Club)

(including New Era and Wheatcroft) and then re-badged them under his own name. In actual fact, all the above is correct. As well as offering cycles made from 'All-British Material' in the assembly of his motorcycles, Lynes used Hobart-made frames and fitted them with various capacity Villiers, JAP and Blackburne power units selling from £48. These overhead-valve Blackburne models were the most powerful of the range, and according to the company, were 'specially built for Hill-climbs and Speed'.
(See also New Era, and Wheatcroft.)

ALERT, 1903–1912 (1882–1955)
Smith & Molesworth Ltd, Freeth Street Mills, 26 Freeth Street

When Smith and Molesworth first joined forces in the late nineteenth century, few would have predicted that their company would still be in business over seventy years later, but that's exactly what happened. John Molesworth was born in Coventry in 1846, and George Smith in 1840 in nearby Nuneaton. After working for many years as separate elastic web manufacturers, in 1882 they set up business together as 'Elastic Web and Cycle Manufacturers' at Freeth Street, Coventry. By 1903 they had diversified into building motor-bicycles powered by 2¼hp Sarolea engines, which were to develop in design over the coming years to a very high quality. Along with other similar companies, the First World War was to have an impact on business, but they survived, concentrating on cycle manufacture thereafter under the Directorship of George Molesworth and H. Reesby. This was to prove a good move for Smith & Molesworth Ltd, because the company continued up to 1955 as 'Cycle Factors for the Trade'.
(See also Ayton-Riley.)

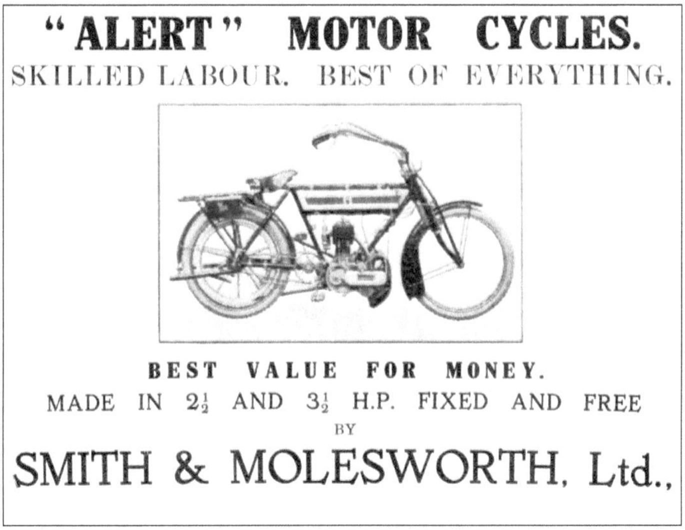

Smith & Molesworth's advertisment for the 'Alert' machine. (Coventry Transport Museum)

ALLARD, 1898–1902 (1890–1902)
Allard & Co. Ltd, 42 Moor Street, & Earlsdon Works, Osborne Road, Earlsdon

In 1885, a gentleman by the name of William Pitt bought a plot of land at Moor Street, Earlsdon, and had a factory constructed to manufacture industrial nails. Pitt's business proved to be an environmental nuisance to the Earlsdon residents, so in 1889/90 Pitt was forced to vacate, and Allard & Co. were established there selling 'Royal Allard' cycles. The firm was founded by 26-year-old Frederick W. Allard of Northampton, a keen cycle racer and former 'Safety Champion of the World'. Also involved in the running of the business was Arthur Pilkington of Birmingham, who, together with Allard, had spent many years working at the Coventry Machinists Co. By 1898, Allard & Co. had steadily progressed to produce a car and a motorised

Frederick W. Allard – former 'Safety Champion of the World'. (Coventry Transport Museum)

F.W. Allard on his very own Allard motorcycle. (Coventry Transport Museum)

tricycle, both being exhibited at Crystal Palace. In 1901 they built their first motorcycle, fitted with a 1¾hp engine, which was later increased to 2hp, and Allard himself was known to have raced a modified version of this in competitions. Later that year, business associates the Birmingham Motor Manufacturing Co. took over Allard, creating a new enterprise called the Rex Motor Manufacturing Co. at larger works on Osborne Road. This takeover involved the Pilkington and Williamson brothers, yet this was not the end of Fred Allard. Enjoying a new life as a publican in Coventry, he also represented the Rex Co. on the national racing circuit for the next few seasons. Later, in 1922, the Coventry Acme Motor Co. were seen to be marketing 'Allard' cycles, yet whether Fred Allard was actually involved in the creation of this firm, which began in 1902 at the Osborne Road address, is not clear.
(See also Coventry Acme, and Rex.)

ALPHA, 1907–1908 (1901–1950)
Johnson, Hurley & Martin, Gosford Street

Messrs Johnson, Hurley and Martin had all previously worked at the Daimler Motor Co. as engineers and motor fitters before deciding to set up their own engineering concern in 1901 at humble premises in Gosford Street. This kind of opportunism was very common at the time, with many individuals looking to make money from an industry on the up, and fully utilising the experience gained under others. What followed was the introduction of the Alpha car later that year, and a motorcycle of the same name by 1907/8. The company then concentrated on car production until the First World War began, before specialising in general engineering until closure in 1926. In 1927, the company reformed as Alpha Engineering Ltd at Osborne Road, Earlsdon, making petrol engines for industrial use. By 1950 the company was still going strong – and being run by the descendants of Hurley and Martin.

ARC, 1911–1913

Auto Repairs Co., 5 Lincoln Street, Bishopsgate Green

Leicester-born Albert E. Gilbert made the short move to Coventry during the latter phases of the nineteenth century, where he found employment as a 'Mechanic in the cycle trade'. The cycle company he initially worked for is so far unknown, yet the 1901 census may provide an indication. Listed is a 49-year-old Mr George Gilbert of Coventry, working as a 'Cycle Manufacturer'. George Gilbert was the founder of the Centaur Cycle Co. along with Edward Mushing from 1876, but interestingly they had started building their own motorcycles from 1901 until 1910. Mushing died in that year, and at this point they were then taken over by the Humber Co. Considering this, and the dates concerned, George Gilbert could well have been the father or uncle of Albert. Nevertheless, in 1911 Albert had set up the Auto Repairs Co. at Lincoln Street as a 'cycle and motor expert' in premises previously occupied by Coventry Eagle and Challenge. It was during this time that he produced a motorcycle in order to expand the company, but it was not a commercial success and the Auto Repairs Co. lasted only two years.

ARNO, 1906–1915

Arno Motor Co., Arno Motor Works, 85–86 Gosford Street & Hill Cross

The Arno Motor Co. was founded in premises inside Court 33, Gosford Street, backing on to the rear of the 'Humber no. 5 Works'. Production started off in a small way in 1906 with motorcycles fitted with 3½hp sleeve-valve engines, before later going on to produce TT specification and touring models. These machines really stood out as they were all finished in bright colours, including an 'All Purple Arno-de-Luxe' version. Between 1908 and 1911, Arno diversified into building modest motorcars, and by 1913 the company had moved to premises at Hill Cross. At this point the Gosford Street Works were taken over by the Regent Motor Sidecar Co. and Hotchkiss & Co., the artillery manufacturers. Unfortunately, nothing is known about the men behind the Arno Motor Co.

(See also Red Arno.)

The 1911 Arno TT model. (Mortons Media)

An Arno machine of 1914, a year before the company closed. (Mortons Media)

An Atlas motorcycle of 1919. (Vintage Motor Cycle Club)

ATLAS, 1913–1920 (1913–1939)

Atlas Engineering Co., Stoneleigh Works, Hill Street

In 1913, the Atlas Engineering Co. was established at Stoneleigh Works, Hill Street – a stone's throw from the huge Leigh Mills weaving factory. Primarily a general engineering firm, Atlas tried their hand at motorcycle production and built machines assembled from various outsourced components for touring and TT specification, finished in black and red. They were fitted with either JAP or Blumfield single-cylinder 500cc engines until 1920 and were said to appeal mainly to 'speed merchants'. Unlike many, they were fortunate to survive the First World War, yet perhaps the economic after-effects were too substantial, forcing closure soon after. The man behind the firm is revealed in the 1939 Coventry Directory – A.J.E. Wain. This refers to Arthur John Edward Wain, born in Nottingham in 1882.

AURORA, 1902–1905

Aurora Motor Manufacturing Co., 12 Norfolk Street, Spon End

In 1902, a gentleman by the name of Charles Bourquin set up the Aurora Motor Manufacturing Co. at Norfolk Street, Coventry. Bourquin, a Swiss foreign national, had arrived in the city a few years earlier, finding work as a watchmaker, yet must have also had a background in

The Aurora motor-bicycle of 1902–1905 had a tendency to skid. (Vintage Motor Cycle Club)

engineering in order to turn his hand to motor assembly. His chosen address was formerly occupied by a Mr John Basnett, a 'Watch-Mover Maker', the entire terrace being purpose built for the Coventry watch industry, which was by now in steep decline. Bourquin began by building a 2½hp 'Aurora' motor-bicycle and later a 3½hp forecar on a very limited scale. He used a variety of engines in his machines, most of which were in fact Coventry-built, including MMC, Condor, Coronet and Whitley. This small company only survived three years, probably due to the fact that their motorcycles apparently had a tendency to 'skid quite freely'. For more details of Bourquin, see *Coventry's Motorcar Heritage*.

AYTON-RILEY, 1907

Smith & Molesworth, 26 Freeth Street
Riley Engine Co., Aldbourne Road

In 1906, the Riley Engine Co. decided to cease the manufacture of motorcycles and concentrate on motorcars, which they did quite successfully until 1969. In the years preceding this, a Mr Robert Charles Ayton joined the Coventry Motorcycle Club where he met fellow members Victor, Allan and Stanley Riley. Ayton was born in London in 1871, and sometime during the last decade of the nineteenth century he moved to Coventry and found employment at the Roulette Cycle Co. Soon afterwards he became a clerk for the Triumph Cycle Co., and, being a keen motorcyclist, often represented Triumph in competitions. On meeting the Riley brothers, Ayton tried to convince them to make bigger and faster machines as he had his sights on entering the first ever Isle of Man Tourist Trophy race the following year. Although winding down motorcycle production, Victor Riley took him up on the idea and built a 5hp Vindec Special Twin, and soon after, a Riley 'Six'. Ayton tested the machines and liked their performance, but being quite short in stature he would need the machine to be specially built for his size. He again approached the Riley Engine Co. and asked for help, but was reminded

Robert Ayton entered his machine into the first Isle of Man TT race in 1907. (Mortons Media)

that they no longer manufactured motorcycles, having committed the sale on all the machinery needed to do so. Instead, Riley pointed Ayton in the direction of Smith & Molesworth. This company had carried out work for Riley before and had also built their own 'Alert' motorcycles from 1903. The result was a tailor-made frame by Smith & Molesworth, powered by a 3½hp race-prepared Riley air-cooled engine, with purpose-built extended handlebars. It was registered DU 931 and was indeed entered in the 1907 Tourist Trophy. Ayton finished 7th overall and won a £5 prize for fuel economy, averaging 117 miles per gallon. Although doing remarkably well in his first ever international race, Riley did not see enough potential to begin the manufacture of motorcycles again.
(See also Alert, and Riley.)

BARBURY & DOWNES
(See Coventry B&D, Coventry B&S, Three Spires, and Wee McGregor.)

BAYLISS, THOMAS & CO.
(See Excelsior.)

BEESTON, 1896–1901
New Beeston Cycle Co. Ltd, Parkside, Cheylesmore

When Harry J. Lawson first decided to stake a claim on the British motor industry, few would have predicted just how much of an impact he and his companies would have. In 1896, the New Beeston Cycle Co. Ltd, which began with a huge nominal capital of £1m, was just the second of Lawson's newly floated companies. Obtaining licenses to use De Dion-Bouton patents, Beeston made 1¼hp tricycles at works at Park Side, premises that were later to be used by Maudslay and Swift. Lawson's prospectus for the new company stated that 'miles of benches were to be erected for the production of bicycles and motorcycles'. In the first London to Brighton run of November 1896, the only English participant was in fact a 1¼hp Beeston tricycle, a copy of the De Dion-Bouton tricycle, but significant in that it was one of the first motorized vehicles to be made in Coventry. In 1898, under the management of Samuel Gorton, they produced quadricycles and chain-driven motor-bicycles with engines mounted over the front wheel. By 1901 the company closed, but because of its close links to Lawson, and in-turn, Humber, much of the Beeston workforce quickly found suitable employment.
(See also Gorton, and Lawson.)

A Beeston tricycle of 1897. (Coventry Transport Museum)

BOOTH BROS

(See Kenilworth.)

BRITISH CHALLENGE, 1919–1920 (1901–1933)

British Challenge Cycle Co. Challenge Works, 201 Foleshill Road, Bishopsgate Green

The Challenge Cycle Co. were established as cycle makers at 24 Bishop Street in 1901, late starters in a city whose cycle origins can be traced back to 1868. They produced their first motor-bicycle under the 'Coventry Challenge' name just two years later at larger premises on Foleshill Road. In 1919/20, the company produced 'carrier' cycles and limited two-stroke motorcycles under the new company name of British Challenge, but for unknown reasons switched back to the name of Coventry Challenge soon after.
(See also Challenge, and Coventry Challenge.)

CAESAR, 1922–1923 (1897–1929)

Caesar Cycle Co. Ltd, 36 Hertford Street, & 37 Clarendon Street, Earlsdon

The Caesar Cycle Co. was founded in 1897 at 36 Hertford Street by William Jones. They produced bicycles there and at works at Clarendon Street, Earlsdon until 1929. At this time, Earlsdon had grown considerably and was home to many other related companies including Coventry Bicycles Ltd, New Era and Rex-Acme. Whilst at this address, Caesar also produced lightweight motorcycles using 269cc Villiers two-stroke engines in an attempt to bolster falling cycle sales, but ultimately did not succeed in doing so. Jones later concentrated on the exportation of motors until around 1929.
(See also Jones, W.M.)

W. Jones began by manufacturing 'Caesar' cycles from 1897. (Vintage Motor Cycle Club)

CALCOTT, 1905–1915 (1886–1926)

Calcott Bros Ltd, 132–134 Much Park Street & 165 Gosford Street

The company of Calcott Bros Ltd began as Calcott Bros & West at East Street in 1886. The Calcott brothers were William and James, both born in Radford, Coventry in 1847 and 1850 respectively. The other side of the partnership was Enoch John West, who left in 1891 to form his own cycle company, E.J. West & Co. Ltd, and a few years later, the Progress Cycle Co. On his departure, the business was re-established as Calcott Bros Ltd under the Directorship of William Calcott Jnr, specialising in the 'XL' machine, and this would later become the name of their works on Gosford Street. By 1905, they had started experimenting with motorcycles but did not seriously enter the market until 1910/11, with 3½hp machines using Coventry-built White & Poppe engines. Calcott also began making cars from 1913 and this is where they ultimately concentrated their efforts until being taken over by the Singer Motor Co. in 1926. Later accounts of the Calcott brothers reveals two very different personalities. According to Triumph founder Siegfried Bettmann in his autobiography *Struggling*, he states that James Calcott was 'a devout nonconformist and would quote the Bible at any given opportunity', while William Calcott 'liked a glass of beer or whiskey and died a fairly young man in rather distressing circumstances'.

(See also Progress.)

The striking façade of the Calcott Works, which still stands to this day. (Coventry Transport Museum)

The Calcott Works iron foundry in 1921. (Coventry Transport Museum)

CENTAUR, 1901–1915 (1876–1915)

Centaur Cycle Co. Ltd, 59 West Orchard
Centaur Co. Ltd, Humber Road, Stoke

The Centaur Cycle Co. was established at West Orchard in 1876 by Edward Mushing and George Gilbert. Gilbert, born in 1852, apprenticed at the celebrated art metal worker Francis Skidmore's in Coventry before joining the Coventry Machinists Co. Mushing, born in 1843, had been for many years a Coventry schoolmaster yet resigned the position to start the Centaur business with Gilbert, and between them they established a very reputable cycle company, registering the 'Centaur' bicycle by 1886. By this time the firm were also producing tricycles, rowing apparatus, roller skates, and, bizarrely, tennis rackets. As early as 1901, Centaur began producing chain-driven motor-bicycles, powered by 3hp Humber engines, and exhibited these for the first time at the 1902 National Show. By 1904, they began to use their own engines, claiming 'the difficulty of starting and the possibility of a back fire to the discomfort of the rider is entirely overcome'. In 1910 Mushing died, and the business was taken on by the Humber Co., who moved production to their new factory at Stoke, Coventry. Also in 1910, two 3½hp Centaur machines were entered in the Isle of Man TT, which was gaining popularity each year. One ridden by F.W. Chase finished in 29th position, but the other rider, F.W. Applebee, was forced to retire. Humber produced the Centaur models practically as replicas of their own until 1915 before dropping the name altogether.

(See also Humber.)

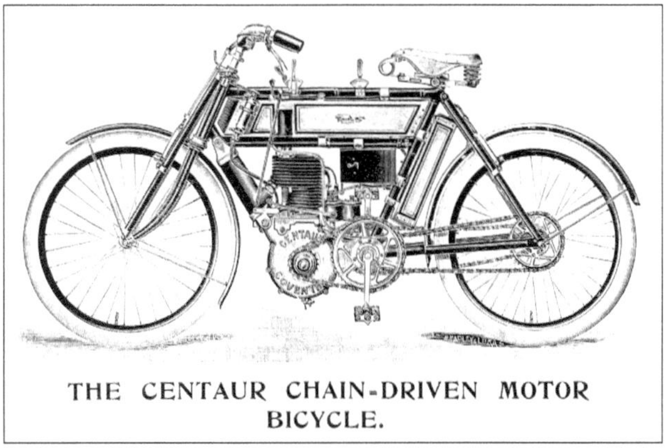

Advertisment for a 1904 Centaur motor-bicycle. (Coventry Transport Museum)

Staff at the Challenge Cycle Co. with Edward O'Brien pictured third from the left. (Coventry Transport Museum)

CHALLENGE, 1911–1913 (1903–1933)

Challenge Motor Co., Challenge Works, 201 Foleshill Road, Bishopsgate Green

Although the Challenge Motor Co. used Coventry Challenge as their main marque in motorcycle production, they also built machines using only the 'Challenge' name at their Foleshill Road Works from 1911 to 1913. They also used the 'British Challenge' marque for the 1919/20 season, before once again reverting back to the name that the buying public were more accustomed to.

(See also British Challenge, and Coventry Challenge.)

CLARENDON, 1901–1911

Hammon & Smith, Dale Street
Clarendon Motor Car & Cycle Co. Ltd, 77 Moor Street, Earlsdon

Messrs Hammon and Smith joined forces in 1901 to form the Clarendon Motor Car & Cycle Co. Ltd. Starting out at small premises in Dale Street alongside the Hamilton Motor Co.,

Hammon & Smith's Clarendon motorbicycles were manufactured from 1901 using Coventry-built engines. (Coventry Transport Museum)

they built cycles, motor-bicycles and cars. Their primitive yet well-made motorcycles were fitted with Coventry-manufactured engines including Hamilton, Birch, Whitley and Coronet. On moving to larger works at Moor Street, Earlsdon in 1903, the Coronet Motor Co. took over the running of Clarendon, but due to financial difficulties they made no more complete motorcycles after 1911. It is not certain who the men behind Clarendon actually were, but it would be safe to assume that both previously worked together in Coventry at a large cycle or car company such as Daimler, before transferring their engineering skills to a company of their own.

CLARKE, CLULEY & CO.

(See Globe.)

CMM, 1918–1921 (1918–1962)

Coventry Motor Mart Ltd, 86 London Road & 5–6 Whitefriars Street

Established in 1918 at London Road by Richard and Cyril Lord, the Coventry Motor Mart were primarily in the business of being distributors of various makes of motorcycles, specialising in the Birmingham-built BSA and James marques among others right up until 1962. However, they were also experienced mechanical engineers and at the beginning of the business sold modified lightweight 2¾hp, 292cc Union-powered machines re-badged under the CMM

Richard Lord pictured during his days employed by the Rex Co. (Coventry Transport Museum)

Cyril Lord made a name for himself in Speedway when the sport first came to Britain. (Coventry Transport Museum)

brand. By the 1950s, Coventry Motor Mart Ltd had four separate divisions in the city – cycle, motorcycle and car sales, plus a domestic electrical side. Cyril Lord went on to become a notable Speedway rider in Coventry from 1928. Dick Lord (b. 1888) was a former rider and senior employee of Coventry-based Rex in their early days. Between 1909 and 1911 he raced a Rex machine at the Isle of Man TT, but each time unfortunately failed to complete the course. It was during this time that he met, and later married, Muriel Hind, the pioneering female motorcyclist. The couple resided at Wall Hill Hall in Corley, on the outskirts of Coventry, until the 1960s.
(See also Rex.)

Muriel Hind (1882–1956)

Agnes Muriel Hind first found notoriety in the early 1900s, when she reputedly became the first woman in Britain to own and ride a motorcycle, and soon after, compete in national motorcycle trials and races with great success, often overshadowing many of her male competitors.

Hind was born into a wealthy Dorset family on 27 May 1882, but was orphaned at the age of 7 and raised by close relatives at Swanage. One such relative was her Uncle Edward, himself being one of England's pioneer motorcyclists and owner of a Werner machine.

Muriel became a keen cyclist during her teenage years, but was to become more and more interested in motorised transport as time went by. After learning of her brother, 'Norrie' S. Hind's purchase of a motorcycle, she began looking for one herself. Through extensive research the Singer Co. of Coventry stood out in that they were offering a motorised bicycle powered by a 2hp Perks & Birch 'Motor Wheel'. This machine had a dropped frame that allowed a long skirt to not impose on riding, so on her 21st birthday in May 1903, she collected the Singer from her Bournemouth dealer – the Birmingham & Coventry Motor Co. Shortly afterwards, Hind relocated to Coventry due to its growing involvement in the motor industry.

As a lady, Hind was determined to cycle in a graceful manner and adopted a style that became closely associated with her – a hat held in place with a tulle scarf, an ankle length tweed coat and skirt, gauntlet gloves and lace-up knee boots. In case of bad weather, she always packed a lightweight waterproof overall that was often brought into use.

Her second motorcycle was a 2½hp Singer, soon followed by a 3hp chain-driven version of which she is said to have enjoyed 8,000 trouble-free miles upon. Although it was unheard of for women, Hind was eager to become involved in motorcycle competitions so in early 1905 she became a member of the Motor Cycling Club. Her first competitive ride came in October 1905 for the Albert Brown Trophy – a 100-mile non-stop run incorporating a hill climb and break test of which she was awarded a token certificate, losing out to overall winner Mr R.M. Brice. In this year Hind also added a Deasy car and a Singer tri-car to her collection of vehicles.

The year 1906 saw a string of successes including a Gold Medal at the Automobile Cycle Club for London to Edinburgh 24-hours Run, followed by a Bronze Medal at the six-day run from Land's End to John O'Groats, both in 9hp Singer tri-cars.

As a liberated female motorist, Hind at times broke the rules and often found herself up before a judge. One such occasion came about whilst taking part in a reliability trial where she was charged with driving a motorcycle in a manner dangerous to the public and was fined £2.

While taking part in trials and competitions, more manufacturers began to look towards building machines that catered for female riders, and Muriel Hind began testing many of these models and reviewing them in the motorcycle press. One such company that wanted to break into the female motorcycle market was the Coventry-based Rex Motor Manufacturing Co., and in late 1907 they created the 'Blue Devil' to a design specified by Hind.

Muriel Hind during an outing, pre-First World War. As a pioneering female motorcyclist she inspired and encouraged other women to take up motoring. (Coventry Transport Museum)

Muriel Hind became a respected motoring journalist, and reviewed many machines tailored for the female market. (Coventry Transport Museum)

Muriel married Richard Lord of the Rex Co. in 1912 – pictured here on a Rex TT motorcycle. (Coventry Transport Museum)

Muriel Hind became instantly recognisable through her customised dress when motoring. (Coventry Transport Museum)

In January of 1908, at the ACU Quarterly Trail, Hind raced to victory in horrendous weather, beating Frank Applebee (on a 5hp Rex) and Jack Marshall (on a 3½hp Triumph) to 2nd and 3rd places, causing great media attention in the racing fields.

From 1910 Hind became more active in writing – notably in a fortnightly column entitled 'The Lady Motorcyclist', influencing more and more women to take up motoring.

Through her business dealings with the Rex Motor Co., Muriel became friendly with Richard Lord who held a senior position at the firm. 'Dick', as he was commonly known, was heavily active in promoting their machines through trials and exhibitions, one of which was a John O'Groats to Land's End run staged in 1906, various trials, hill climbs and twice entrant in the Isle of Man TT during 1909–1911. After many years working closely together, Muriel married Dick Lord at Paddington, London in 1912.

Following their marriage, both decided to retire from competitive racing, yet still kept active. Muriel concentrated more on journalism, writing motoring reviews and articles. In 1915 she gave birth to a son, Brian. Along with his brother Cyril, Dick Lord established the Coventry Motor Mart Co. after the First World War, specialising in selling James motorcycles.

In 1931 Muriel Lord became the first woman to be elected a life member of the Association of Pioneer Motor Cyclists, and in 1950 became an honorary life member of the Motor Cycle Club.

They resided at the pleasant Wall Hill Hall in rural Corley, near Coventry, yet always maintained their interest in cars and motorcycles. In 1952 Harold Karslake reported that they still regularly drove a Singer Le Mans sports car, an Austin saloon, a 1914 Douglas motorcycle, and Muriel's famous 'Blue Devil' Rex. Another 5hp Rex motorcycle had been 'robbed' of its engine some thirty-five years earlier to power a lawnmower that was still going strong.

Such was her energy that at the age of 56 Muriel cycled to Oxford and back in a single day – a round trip of some 120 miles! She endured many accidents during her racing career, yet a fall at her Wall Hill Hall home in 1954 subsequently confined her to a wheelchair.

Muriel died on 3 May 1956 at the age of 74, four years before her husband. She will be remembered for being the first woman in Britain, and possibly the world, to own and ride a motorcycle, and through her outstanding competitive achievements in a male-dominated sport and pastime, as well as her inspirational writing, she opened up the way for many more women to become involved in motoring.

Richard and Muriel pictured in Warwickshire on a Rex combination. (Coventry Transport Museum)

Wall Hill Hall on the outskirts of Coventry became their family home. (Coventry Transport Museum)

CONDOR, 1907–1924 (1907–1955)

Condor Motor Co. Ltd, 182–184 Broad Street Garage, Great Heath

The Condor Motor Co. Ltd began life as 'Engine Makers and Motor Engineers', but also produced motorcycles from 1907, and cycle cars on a limited scale in 1913. Their machines were quite powerful for their time, fitted with 650cc and 800cc engines by 1912. By 1920 they became the Condor Motor & Fittings Co. Ltd, specialising in 'aero-engine valves', yet still offering motorcycles until 1924. By 1936 they were still based at Broad Street, yet concentrating on 'replacement parts for railway and passenger transport'. At this point their Directors were E. Sidwell and A.E. Sidwell, a surname that was very active in the Coventry cycle industry, and the probable founders of this company. After 1955, to date nothing else has been found concerning the business.

CORONET, 1903–1906 (1896–1910)

Coronet Motor Co. Ltd, 83–87 Far Gosford Street

Like so many Coventry companies of the time, Coronet were initially founded as cycle manufacturers. Their start began in 1896 by Leopold Harris at former watch-making premises in Hearsall Lane, Chapelfields. By 1903 they had relocated to much larger works at Far Gosford Street, primarily producing cars, as well as motor-bicycles in small quantities, under the design of Brighton-born Walter Iden (b. 1873) as Chief Engineer. Iden was the son of George Iden of Lawson's Motor Manufacturing Co., and also formed his own car company under the 'Iden' name in Coventry, based at Fleet Street from 1904–1907. The Coronet Motor Co. itself was also known to have supplied engines on a limited scale to firms such as Crypto and Jones. In 1906, they fell into difficulties and were said to have been taken over by Humber, but by 1910 the entire operation was dropped and the factory was converted into housing.
(See also MMC.)

COVENTRY, 1910–1911 (1901–1911)

Harris Cycle Co., Hill Cross House, Upper Well Street

Another Coventry bicycle concern, the Harris Cycle Co. was established in Upper Well Street around 1901 in a building known as Hill Cross House. One of the men known to have been involved was Coventry-born Walter Tatlow, a company Director and Sergeant in the Royal Warwickshire Regiment. Another may well have been Leopold Harris of the Coronet Motor Co., which closed in 1910. After around seven years of cycle building, the Harris management decided to enter the motorcycle market with a basic 3½hp belt-driven model, but considering the whole enterprise failed the following year, it would seem that this was not the best of moves. Hill Cross House was initially built as a private residence in the nineteenth century, but was adapted for industrial use some years later. Like many buildings in Coventry, it was sadly demolished in the 1960s to make way for the ring road, the relevant section of which has been aptly named 'Hill Cross'.

COVENTRY ACME, 1920–1922

Coventry Acme Motor Co. Ltd, Earlsdon Cycle Works, Osborne Road, Earlsdon

The Acme Motor Co. was founded at Osborne Road, Coventry in 1902. After the war in 1920 they changed their company name to Coventry Acme for a brief period, producing two-speed 292cc single-cylinder motorcycles under the same name, as well as 'Allard' cycles. They also introduced their 8hp 'Acme-Jap' big twin model, reported at the time as a 'promising passenger

outfit'. The business was forced to change its name a final time just two years later, merging with the Rex Motor Co. to become Rex-Acme. Whether Frederick Allard was actually connected to the Acme Co. or simply sold the trade name is unclear.
(See also Acme, Allard, Rex, and Rex-Acme.)

COVENTRY B&D, 1923–1926 (1918–1936)

Coventry Bicycles Ltd, Barbury & Downes, Roulette Works, 85–86 Gosford Street, Wellington Street, Priory Street & Osborne Road, Earlsdon

Messrs Barbury and Downes were former employees of the Hobart Cycle & Motorcycle Co. before being appointed Managers of this cycle firm at Gosford Street in 1918 by Triumph co-founder Siegfried Bettmann. A year later, they began the sale of motorcycles under the name of the 'Wee McGregor', a lightweight 170cc machine. By 1923 they also introduced the Coventry B&D and Coventry B&S ranges at new premises at Wellington Street. These machines were assembled using various sized capacity JAP engines, with the exception of the Coventry B&S, which stood for Barr & Stroud. In 1924, four Coventry B&D machines were offered by the firm, ranging from 346cc to 876cc. Later, in 1931, Coventry Bicycles Ltd introduced the 'Three Spires' motorcycle. Coventry Bicycles Ltd traded as such until 1936 when it was restructured as the Associated Cycle Manufacturers of Coventry Ltd.
(See also Coventry B&S, Three Spires, Triumph, Wee McGregor, and White Heather.)

A Coventry B&D motorcycle of 1923. (Vintage Motor Cycle Club)

Barbury and Downes built the Coventry B&S for 1923 only. (Mortons Media)

COVENTRY B&S, 1923

Coventry Bicycles Ltd, Barbury & Downes, Wellington Street

This marque was used by Barbury & Downes of Coventry Bicycles Ltd in 1923 only. The B&S stood for Barr & Stroud, the 349cc engine used. The company built motorcycles and cycles at numerous addresses in Coventry between 1923 and 1932.
(See also Coventry B&D, Three Spires, and Wee McGregor.)

COVENTRY CHALLENGE, 1903–1922 (1901–1933)

Challenge Cycle Co. Ltd, Challenge Works, 201 Foleshill Road, Bishopsgate Green

The 'Challenge' name enjoyed nearly thirty years of trade at the Foleshill Road factory, a site that they initially acquired back in 1903 after brief stays at Lincoln Street and Bishop Street. Their main output concerned cycle production, but they began building 'Coventry Challenge' motorcycles also from 1903 onwards. These early machines were powered by Minerva and Fafnir engines, with production overseen by Designer/Manufacturer, Edward Salmon O'Brien, a 'Wholesale and Shipping Cycle & Motor Agent'. After the war, they used 269cc Villiers and JAP engines in their machines until 1922, when they concentrated solely on cycle building. O'Brien's origins are not well recorded, but he worked as a Cycle Dealer in Coventry from around 1900, and a cycle shop of the same name existed on the same site until the 1990s.
(See also British Challenge, and Challenge.)

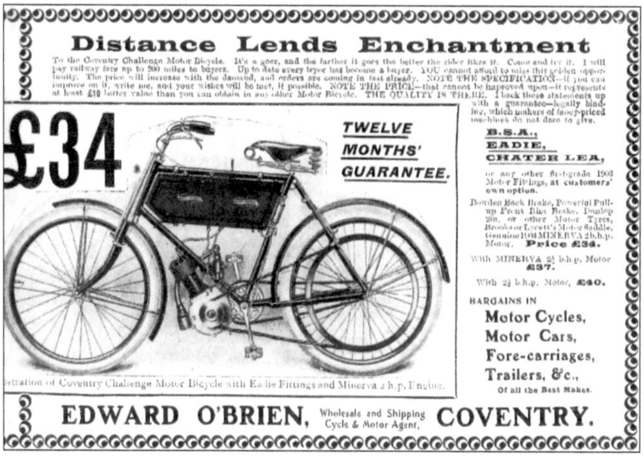

Edward O'Brien offered good terms with his Coventry Challenge machines. (Vintage Motor Cycle Club)

A later Coventry Challenge model of 1919. (Mortons Media)

COVENTRY EAGLE, 1898–1950 (1890–1968)

New Coventry Eagle Co., 4 Lincoln Street, 201 Foleshill Road & St Patrick's Road

Coventry Eagle Cycle & Motor Co., 4 Lincoln Street, 201 Foleshill Road, St Patrick's Road & Duggins Lane

Coventry Eagle marketed their first motorised machine in 1898. (Coventry Transport Museum)

The Coventry Eagle motorcycle was borne out of a cycle company formed by Messrs Hotchkiss, Mayo and Meek in 1890, selling 'Royal Eagle' cycles at their Hill Cross factory. In 1897, Hotchkiss died, John Meek left, and the firm became the Coventry Eagle Cycle Co. under the ownership of Edmund Mayo and Bernard N. Rotherham at Lincoln Street. Mayo was born at Brandon, Warwickshire in 1854. He worked for many years in the Coventry watch industry at Rotherham & Sons as a Clerk before turning to cycle production. By 1898, the company started to build motorised vehicles including a 2¾hp forecar and a motorcycle fitted with a Coventry-made MMC engine. By 1901 they were renamed the New Coventry Eagle Co., continuing the production of cycles, motorcycles fitted with their own and Buchet motors, and 'trailing cars' at their Lincoln Street Works. Before long, Mayo introduced his son, Arthur, to the firm, where he took up the position of Secretary. In 1902 the company's sales catalogue read: 'The motor-bicycle has also received careful attention, and we believe we have produced one of the most elegant, durable, and efficient motor-bicycles yet manufactured'. A few years later, Arthur Mayo's son Percy, who had previously worked at Royal Ordnance as a gun designer, also joined. By 1914, the company were offering sidecars, and motorcycles fitted with 299cc Villiers engines, but the outbreak of war slowed production. Percy went off to serve his country, and whilst out there, met a certain Mr George Brough. It has been reported that after the war they worked together on the first Brough Superior motorcycle, and Mayo was said to be behind the distinctive shape of the tank, similar to some Coventry Eagle machines of the same era. By now, Coventry Eagle had made the short move to 201 Foleshill Road, and were selling V-Twin motorcycles powered by 680cc JAP engines, increased to 976cc by 1923. The mid-1920s saw the company break records at Brooklands with Bert Le Vack being their most successful rider. In 1930 came their well-received 'Flying 8' machine, a 988cc JAP model costing £120, while the company enlarged their factory space to meet growing demand. Production continued steadily into the Second World War, offering the 'Silent Pullman Two-Seater', and by 1940, an autocycle called the 'Auto-Ette'. Fitted with a 98cc engine it was aimed at the lower end of the market, costing just £17. By 1950, only three Coventry motorcycle manufacturers remained: Coventry Eagle, Francis-Barnett, and Triumph, yet this would be the final year that Coventry Eagle would produce a motorcycle. Under the Directorship of further descendants A.G. Kenwrick Mayo and A. Douglas Mayo, they moved one final time to Duggins Lane, Tile Hill. Here they continued to sell cycles until 1968, rounding up a family business in Coventry that had lasted almost eighty years.

(See also Royal Eagle.)

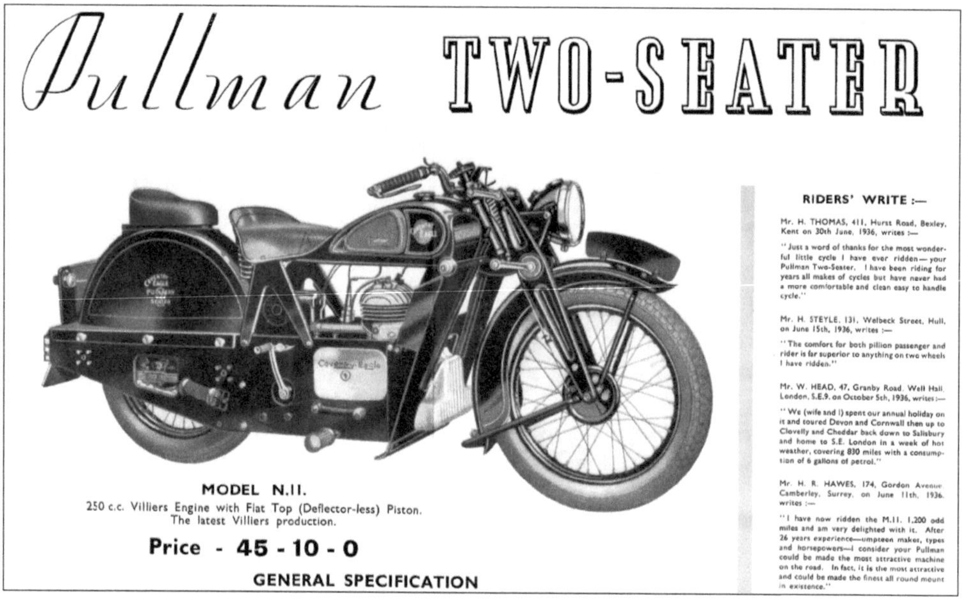

The Pullman model was first released in 1936. (Coventry Transport Museum)

COVENTRY ENSIGN, 1919–1923 (1919–1934)

Coventry Ensign Cycle & Motor Co. Ltd, 201 Foleshill Road, Bishopsgate Green

The Coventry Ensign Cycle & Motor Co. was yet another small post-war manufacturer set up in the city. Starting out from humble beginnings, their address is somewhat significant concerning the city's transport heritage. Historically, 201 Foleshill Road in Bishopsgate Green is an area of land once home to many transport related companies. These included the firms of Beacon, Challenge, Coventry Eagle, Coventry Progress, Mohawk, O'Brien, Quadrant, Remington and Standard. Just across the canal from this site stood the famous 'Motor Mills' of the Daimler Motor Co., which manufactured cars and other vehicles from 1896. Living under their shadow, Coventry Ensign would never reach the heights of the likes of Daimler, yet in 1919 they produced a basic motorcycle fitted with a 292cc Jap engine. This was offered for a few years, before Ensign opted to concentrate on cycle production until closure in 1934. Unfortunately, nothing is known about the people who founded the company.

(See also Coventry Emblem (Motorcycle Mysteries).)

COVENTRY MASCOT, 1922–1924 (1921–1924)

Coventry Mascot Cycle Co., 49 Gresham Street & Camden Street, Stoke

Established as children's cycle manufacturers in 1921, the Coventry Mascot Cycle Co. soon chanced their way into the motorcycle market at their Stoke factory. Such was their optimism, the company even entered a 350cc Bradshaw-powered machine ridden by J.L. Brown in the 1923 Isle of Man Junior TT, but despite a gallant effort, he failed to finish the course. Coventry Mascot also offered machines with 350cc Barr & Stroud and Blackburne engines, but it would seem that their gamble was not to pay off, the factory closing after just two years in 1924. Whether Brown had anything to do with the running of the company is unknown.

Coventry Mascot entered a machine into the 1923 Isle of Man Junior TT. (Mortons Media)

COVENTRY MOTETTE, 1897–1903 (1896–1903)

Coventry Motor Co. Ltd, Parkside, & 16 Conduit Yard, Spon Street

In 1896, Harry J. Lawson, along with many other projects he was involved with, bought the UK rights to the French Leon Bollee tri-cars for a reputed £20,000. After a fire at the Humber factory (another one of his concerns), Lawson established the Coventry Motor Co., having the Humber workforce build British versions of the Bollee design. These 2½hp three-wheelers were designed for the female market and given the name of Coventry Motette. They were developed and built under the supervision of Charles McRobie Turrell in both a factory at Parkside and an address situated off medieval Spon Street known as 'Conduit Yard'. One machine was ridden by Mrs H. DeVeulle, the wife of Jersey Mechanical Engineer Frederick H. DeVeulle, from Coventry to London. On reaching her destination, she was presented with a diamond ring by Lawson; such was the extravagance of the man.
(See also Humber, and Lawson.)

A Coventry Motette with Charles Jarrott driving, and Charles Turrell stood at the far rear (in the cap) on the pavement. (CTM)

COVENTRY MOTOR MART

(See CMM.)

COVENTRY PREMIER, 1914 (1890–1923)

Premier Cycle Co., Read Street

This was a marque used only in 1914 by the Premier Cycle Co., whose origins date back to 1890, when Hillman, Herbert and Cooper established their cycle business. The company also built cars at this address between 1913 and 1923 under the guidance of Works Manager G.W.A. Brown, but motorcycle production ceased altogether in 1920.
(See also Hillman, and Premier.)

COVENTRY PROGRESS

(See Progress.)

COVENTRY REGENT, 1920–1921 (1919–1991)

Coventry Victor Motor Co. Ltd, 137–139 Cox Street
Morton & Weaver, 137–139 Cox Street

The Coventry Victor Motor Co. Ltd of Cox Street had a long history in engineering in the city, which lasted until as recently as 1991. Being primarily engine builders for supply, they also produced complete motorcycles from 1919 onwards, and in 1920 introduced the 'Coventry Regent', fitted with a 688cc Coventry Victor flat-twin engine. These engines had been previously supplied to the Regent Co. of London between 1919 and 1920, but when this was phased out, Coventry Victor instead sold the machines under the Coventry Regent marque. In the same year the company began selling sidecars under the Regent name, at works nearby on Gosford Street.
(See also Coventry Victor, and Regent.)

Coventry Victor employees pose for a photograph during a Godiva Procession. (Coventry Transport Museum)

COVENTRY STAR, 1919–1921

New Star Co., Broad Lane, Tile Hill

The 'Coventry Star' goes way back to the 1890s when a Coventry cycle firm called Hosier & Co. first registered the name. It was reinstated in 1919 by the New Star Co. of Broad Lane, Tile Hill, as a two-speed lightweight model, fitted with 269cc Villiers and Liberty engines, of direct belt-drive. This machine, or similar versions, was also offered under both the 'New Star' and 'Star' marques. Whether Mr Hosier had anything to do with this later business remains a mystery. *(See also New Star, and Star.)*

COVENTRY VICTOR, 1919–1939 (1904–1991)

Coventry Victor Motor Co. Ltd, 137–139 Cox Street, & Humber Avenue

In 1904, W.A. Weaver and T.A. Morton established the beginnings of Coventry Victor, creating the company of Morton & Weaver Ltd at Cox Street as 'engineers & machine toolmakers'. Weaver is thought to have been born in Peterborough, later spending many years in Manchester where he was to become associates with John Siddeley, later of Coventry-based Siddeley-Deasy Motors. Weaver became an astute engineer, experimenting with steam cars and tractors before eventually moving to Coventry. He also had a fascination with aviation, and developed his own 'Ornithoplane' between 1905 and 1910, frequently testing it around the city. In July 1906 it was said to have been the first monoplane type aerofoil to leave the ground under its own power in England, at Hampton-in-Arden, Warwickshire. By 1911, Morton & Weaver added the business of Coventry Victor to their interests. As well as building engines and sidecars, their first motorcycles in 1919 were fitted with 689cc horizontally-opposed sv flat-twin-cylinder engines, which they also supplied to other firms including Ayres, McKechnie and Regent. A 750cc model was entered at the 1921 Brookland's 500-mile race which finished 1st having been ridden by E.W. Parham, and by 1925, a 498cc ohv road version was offered. In 1926 they also began making motorcars including three-wheelers, advertising them as having 'vibrationless engines'. The company produced complete vehicles until around 1939, when they concentrated firmly on general engineering, now under the management of Mr A.N. Weaver, William's son. This was to be a good move, as they profited throughout the war, specialising in internal combustion engines. They were still seen to be trading as engineers by 1963, when they moved to new works at Smiths Industrial Estate, Humber Avenue, no doubt brought on by central Coventry's post-war modernisations. After some ninety years of known trading, the company went into liquidation in June 1991. From 1890 onwards, there was in fact a Victor Cycle Co. based at the Old Gate Works, Cook Street, Coventry, but it's uncertain whether this business was in any way connected.

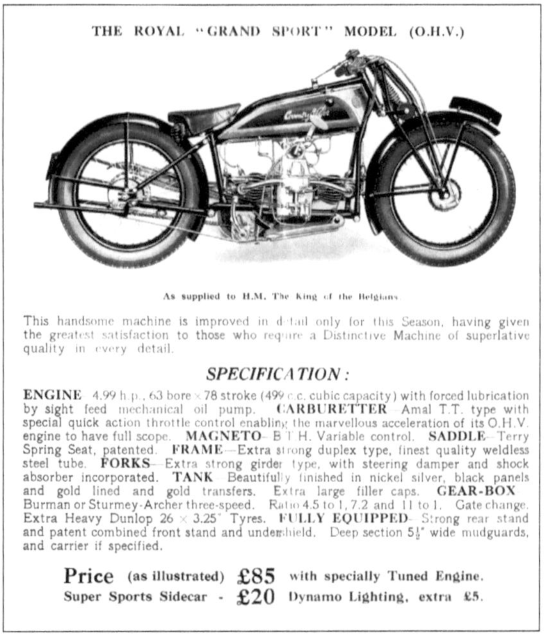

A Coventry Victor Royal Grand Sport model was even supplied to the King of Belgium. (Coventry Transport Museum)

Cameron Croft set himself up in business in 1923. (Coventry Transport Museum)

CROFT-ANZANI, 1923–1926

J.E. Cameron Croft, Harefield Road, Stoke

A make used by Cameron Croft, fitted with a 996cc four- and eight-valve V-Twin engine, of Anzani manufacture. A larger 1,078cc machine was also offered but on a very limited scale. These were machines clearly built by, and for, racing enthusiasts.
(See also Croft-Cameron.)

CROFT-CAMERON, 1923–1926

J.E. Croft-Cameron, St Michaels Road & Harefield Road, Stoke

Like many small motorcycle manufacturers of the 1920s, very little is known about the Croft-Cameron make. Again, like so many others, Cameron Croft was most likely a mechanical engineer specialising in motorcycles, and alongside colleagues developed a motorcycle of their own making. These machines were said to be of similar appearance to Brough models with their trademark saddle tanks, and were fuelled by large 996cc British Anzani V-Twin engines, the 'Super Eight' being their most successful model. Croft had a relatively short life in motorcycle manufacture, lasting only three years.
(See also Croft-Anzani.)

CROMWELL, 1907 (1907–1911)

Cromwell Motor Co., 2 Queen Street, Hillfields

When the Cromwell Motor Co. entered the motorcycle market in 1907, there were already some twenty-five other companies competing for business in Coventry alone. Their start was a modest one, with works at Queen Street being far from adequate in a predominately residential area. The company were largely involved with engine making, yet early on in their short lifespan, they produced a complete motorcycle, with frames most probably supplied from another local firm. It's not known who Cromwell was exactly, but the most likely candidate is William Cromwell of Blackburn, who in 1901 can be seen working in Handsworth, Birmingham, age 25, as a 'Draughtsman to an Engineer'. If this is the man, he would have been aged around 30 by the time he began the Cromwell Motor Co. in Coventry, but nothing is known about his, or the company's activities after 1911.

W.H. Sinnett took a Dart motorcycle to Brooklands in 1923. (Vintage Motor Cycle Club)

DART, 1923–1924

Dart Engineering Ltd, 314a Stoney Stanton Road

Dart Engineering Ltd is yet another company of which very little information exists. All that is known is that in 1923 they set up in premises in Stoney Stanton Road, primarily building engines. In addition to this, they also produced a 349cc single-cylinder motorcycle designed by A.A. Sidney, a former manager of the Birmingham-based Beardmore Co. Later that year, Dart entered one of these machines at Brooklands, ridden by W.H. Sinnett, but unfortunately it failed to perform well. It is not known whether it was Sidney himself who established Dart, but for unknown reasons the business relocated to Bristol in early 1924, lasting for another few months only.

DAVISON, 1902–1907

A.C. Davison Ltd., Viaduct Works, 74 Spon Street

In 1902, Augustine Campbell Davison appeared to have established himself primarily as a motor engineering firm at an industrial address known as 'Viaduct Works' on Spon Street, with an administrative office at 366 Camden Road, London. Yet early on in the company's life, they produced a number of motor bicycles fitted with 2 and 2½ hp Minerva engines as well as other models powered by Simms motors. Originating from Boston, Lincolnshire in 1865, Davison took out a number of motor related patents throughout the course of his elusive

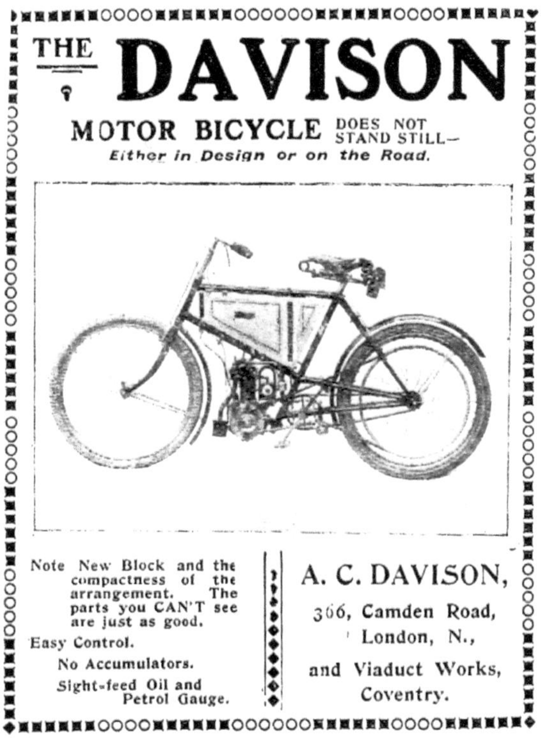

Davison had addresses in both Coventry and London early on. (Vintage Motor Cycle Club)

career, and was known to have been employed for the Birmingham firm of Lucas prior to his coming to Coventry. From 1907, Davison was seen to be working out of a Camden office only, and his activities thereafter remain unknown.

DAW, 1902–1905 (1902–1910)

Dalton & Wade, DAW Motors, 146 Spon Street

Speculation again exists as to who exactly Mr Dalton and Mr Wade were. However, further investigation suggests that one half was Charles Dalton, a Coventry man born in 1871, who earned his initial trade as a 'Motor Fitter'. The other half was Francis Wade, born at Beeston, Nottinghamshire in 1873, who was seen to be working as a 'Mechanical Engineer'. Wade may well have moved to Coventry while working for either the Beeston or Humber companies, both known to have relocated to the city by the 1890s. In 1902, both men found premises at Spon Street and produced motorcycles fitted with their own 1¾, 2¼ and 2¾hp air-cooled engines, as well as 3hp Minerva engines under license from the Belgian company until 1905. They were also known to have supplied engines to other firms including Hobart, before later specialising in general engineering until 1910.

DINGLEY, 1910–1915 (1890–1937)

Dingley Bros, Viaduct Works, 74 Spon Street

Birmingham-born Philip Dingley established Dingley Bros as cycle manufacturers at Spon Street in 1890, registering the 'Starley' bicycle. They quickly earned a solid reputation for making quality machines and were regular exhibitors at the Olympia Show in London. Although their main business activities mostly concerned cycle manufacture, they also produced motorcycles in limited supply. This was cut short in 1915, when the additional expenditure and labour of this venture was cancelled out by the war. The company did survive though, selling bicycles until 1937.

DUX, 1904–1906

Dux Motor Manufacturing Co., Coventry

Dux were yet another company to enter the motor market at the beginning of the twentieth century in Coventry. Their motorcycles were powered by MMC and 3hp Sarolea engines, and the company claimed they had 'the capacity of building fifty complete motorcycles a week' and were the 'Leader of light motors – manufactured entirely in the great motor centre - Coventry'. Like Rex of Earlsdon, the Dux name was of Latin origins, in this case meaning 'Duke'. Another link with the Rex Co. was that they were said to have used Rex-built frames under licence in their motorcycle assembly. An exact address for the Dux Motor Manufacturing Co. has somehow faded from records over time, but considering their close links with Rex, they too may have been Earlsdon based, or even closely tied to the company itself.
(See also MMC, and Rex.)

EXCELSIOR, 1896–1919 (1874–1965)

Bayliss, Thomas & Co., Excelsior Works, Lower Ford Street, Hillfields
Excelsior Motor Co. Ltd, 287 Stoney Stanton Road

The history of the Excelsior motorcycle holds a very proud place in Coventry's transport heritage, with the company reputedly being the first firm in the country to make and sell bicycles

Works rider Harry Martin won many races on the Excelsior machine. (Coventry Transport Museum)

as a commercial operation. Three men were responsible for its origin: Thomas Bayliss of Birmingham (b. 1843), John Thomas of Banbury (b. 1833), and John Slaughter of Aylesbury (b. 1834). All three moved to Coventry when cycle manufacture was in its infancy, and found employment in the industry soon after. Thomas Bayliss, having previously worked in the Birmingham Small Arms trade, found employment at the Coventry Machinists Co. in 1868, alongside the likes of George Singer, James Starley and William Hillman, and thus experienced at first hand the opportunities that this new mode of transport could bring. Two other employees of the Coventry Machinists at this time were Thomas and Slaughter, and so in 1874, these three men came together, setting up as Bayliss, Thomas & Slaughter, building 'Ordinary' cycles in small works at Earl Street and Much Park Street, before finding larger and more suitable premises at 80 Lower Ford Street by 1877. Some time later, Slaughter seems to have parted company, and the firm was re-established as Bayliss, Thomas & Co., continuing to build cycles of high quality for the following years. Whilst doing so, they registered the 'Excelsior' name, taken from a Longfellow poem meaning 'Ever Upward', and by 1878, they were producing some 2,000 cycles a year. In 1896, Bayliss & Thomas began experimenting with motorised vehicles, initially powered by 2¾hp MMC engines. At that point in time, the power of these machines were remarked as being 'unnecessarily fast and powerful', yet these were said to have been the first motorcycles in Great Britain to be marketed. By 1902, the company had exhibited no less than forty Excelsior motorcycles at Olympia in London, the largest amount by any firm. Excelsior machines were also heavily involved in racing competitions early on, notably ridden by Works Manager Harry Martin at venues such as Canning Town and Dublin's Phoenix Park. In 1903, Martin became the first person to reach 60mph whilst covering a mile in just under a minute. By 1905, under the management of Coventry-born William H. Carson, they turned their attention towards developing tri-cars due to comfort issues. In 1909 the company reformed as the Excelsior Motor Cycle Co., and they began building machines fitted with their own 3½hp engines of Carson's design. Between then and the outbreak of the First World War, more than 60 per cent of the company's output was exported consisting of larger machines ranging from 4–5hp of 811cc, to a V-Twin 8hp JAP model. In 1919, Bayliss & Thomas were taken over by R. Walker & Sons and all production moved to Kings Road in Tyseley, Birmingham. At around the same time the company had also begun producing motorcars split between Birmingham and a new site acquired at Stoney Stanton Road, Coventry until 1927. The Excelsior motorcycle continued to be built in Birmingham right the way through to 1965.

(See also MMC.)

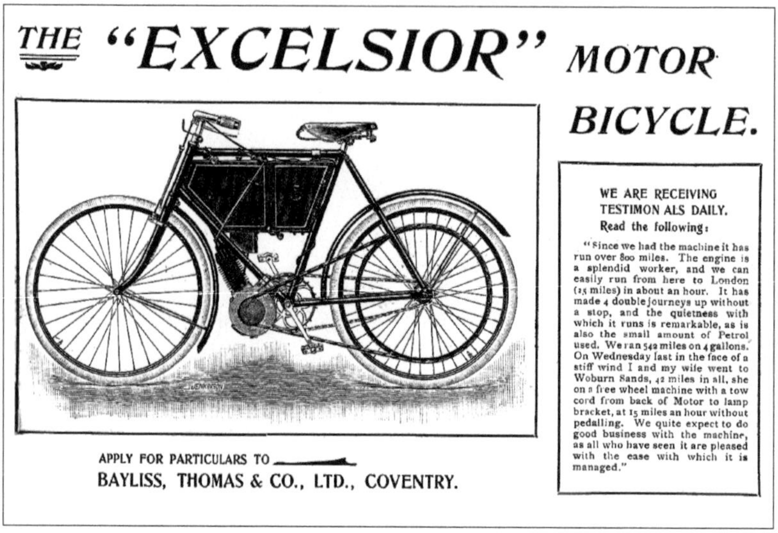

Bayliss, Thomas & Co. were one of the very first to market motor-bicycles in Great Britain. (Coventry Transport Museum)

FRANCIS-BARNETT, 1919–1964 (1919–1968)

Francis-Barnet Ltd, Lower Ford Street, Hillfields

The Francis-Barnett motorcycle, affectionately known as the 'Fanny B', was one of the very last to remain in production in Coventry until 1964. The name began in 1919 when Gordon Francis joined with Arthur Barnett, setting up together at Lower Ford Street at the newly vacant Excelsior Works, the original home of Bayliss, Thomas & Co. The merger was not simply a commercial one, but had a family interest too. Gordon Inglesby Francis was born in Connecticut, America in 1890. He was the son of Graham Francis, who had spent time working in the US for Brown & Sharpe, the machine tool giants, before returning to Coventry to establish Lea-Francis as cycle manufacturers with Richard Lea in 1895. Gordon, known as 'Don', joined Lea-Francis on completing his apprenticeship and went on to develop and road test many of the motorcycles that the company had began to make, establishing himself as a trials rider of some distinction. He was called up for military service in July 1914 and strategically placed in the motorcycle repair depot at St Omer in Northern France. This was to prove a relatively comfortable posting throughout the war, seeing Don return home safely, but much to his father's initial uncertainty, he did not return to work for Lea-Francis. Instead, he opted to start a rival business with his new father-in-law, Arthur Barnett, at premises next door to the Lea-Francis factory. Over time though, Don's father, Graham Francis, became more supportive, cleverly placing himself as Director of the new venture. Coventry-born Arthur Barnett first worked for the Singer Motor Co. before starting his own cycle business, and by 1912 began selling motorcycles under his self-registered 'Invicta' name. By the time he had teamed up with Francis they still marketed the Invicta before concentrating on their own models under the Francis-Barnett marque, their first ones being chain-driven and fitted with 292cc JAP engines. The company went on to become renowned for their new frame concept by 1923. This consisted of seven pairs of tubes that would easily bolt together to form a triangular frame, then fitted to a 147cc Villiers engine. This was sold at a very reasonable price and was promoted by the company as being 'built like a bridge'. Francis-Barnett continued successfully into the 1930s selling lightweight machines called the Pullman, Merlin, Stag and Kestrel of various capacities, keeping faith with the Villiers engine, and maintaining good value for money. Arthur Barnett died in 1937 and his son, Eric A. Barnett replaced

Francis-Barnett

Francis-Barnett specialised in manufacturing lightweight machines. (Coventry Transport Museum)

The Francis-Barnett Cruiser 39 was introduced in 1933. (Coventry Transport Museum)

him as Sales Director, with Don Francis remaining as Technical Director. In the early 1950s they were taken over by Associated Motorcycles Ltd (AMC), one of many amalgamations intended to strengthen the by now failing industry which had increasingly struggled under foreign competition. Disaster rocked the company in 1953 when Eric Barnett was killed in a road accident. It was reported that while on his way home to Southam from work one winters evening, he stopped his car near Princethorpe to make a phone call. On crossing the road he was hit and killed by a lorry which failed to stop – the driver apparently never being traced. By 1957, Francis-Barnett took the decision to use their own AMC engines, but these lacked the reliability of the Villiers units. Through lack of sales and a depleting reputation they switched back to the faithful Villiers in 1962, but by now, Japanese machines were taking a stronghold throughout the country. In 1964 the Lower Ford Street factory was closed and moved to Birmingham, signalling the end of motorcycle production in central Coventry. Despite the move, Francis-Barnett motorcycles lasted only a further four years.

(See also Invicta, and Lea-Francis.)

The Cruiser was one of the company's best-selling models. (Coventry Transport Museum)

GAMAGE, 1919–1923

W.J. Green, Croft Road

Gamage was a famous department store based in Holborn, London, which first opened in 1878. By 1903, they began selling motorcycles, made by other British manufacturers but re-badged in the Gamage name. In 1919, they arranged the sale of machines built by W.J. Green of Coventry. At this time, Green had just established a company of his own, producing engines and motorcycles under the 'Omega' name at an address in Croft Road. This arrangement between Gamage and Green lasted some four years until 1923, but Omega motorcycles continued to be built until 1927. *(See also Omega.)*

GLOBE, 1901–1911 (1884–1987)

Clarke, Cluley & Co., Globe Works, 14 Well Street

Clarke, Cluley & Co. were established as cycle makers at Well Street in 1884. The business was founded by Mr Ernest Clarke of Gloucester and Coventry-born Charles J. Cluley. Cluley was born in 1866, a short time before the first cycles were produced in the city. On leaving school he learned his trade in the industry, joining Clarke and establishing his own company at the young age of 18. Others known to have worked for the company were George Storo Smith, Cycle Manufacturer; George Clarke, Blacksmiths Labourer; John H. Fretton, Clerk; and James D. Blakemore, General Metal Worker. By 1901, the firm added motor-bicycles and forecars to their output, these being powered by their own 2½hp engines, and 3½hp Minerva, MMC and Sarolea engines. After 1911, they once again concentrated on cycle production, but by 1921 began the manufacture of motorcars until 1928. They then became general engineers and by 1934 a producer of parts for textile machinery until their factory was bombed during the Blitz of 1940. A new factory was built at Kenilworth a year later where the company became involved with Aero engineering until closure in 1987. Charles Cluley is buried in the London Road cemetery in Coventry, in a section heavily populated with others associated with the city's transport heritage.
(See also MMC.)

Globe built forecars as well as motor-bicycles. (Vintage Motor Cycle Club)

The Triumph Co. built Gloria motorcycles from 1931. (Mortons Media)

GLORIA, 1931–1933

Triumph Engineering Co., Priory Street & Dale Street

When Siegfried Bettmann and Mauritz Schulte first moved to Coventry in 1887, they established both the Triumph Cycle Co. and the Gloria Cycle Co. in Earls Court, Much Park Street and, later, Priory Street. Triumph excelled and was to become one of the largest and most successful cycle, motorcycle and car companies in the country. In 1931, as well as selling Triumph motorcycles in their own name, they also re-introduced the Gloria marque, brought back from their early cycle days. The Gloria was a basic lightweight model, aimed at the lower end of the market. It was fitted with an economical 98cc Villiers engine, and by 1933 a 147cc model was offered. Triumph also used the Gloria name in the production of cars and sidecars.

(See also Triumph.)

GODIVA, 1900–1901 (1890–1934)

Payne & Bates Ltd, Godiva Street, Castle Street & Foleshill Road

A true Coventry name for a product if ever there was one, the 'Godiva' was introduced in 1900 by Walter Payne and George Bates, the men behind Payne & Bates Ltd. Walter Samuel Payne was born in 1863 in Thrapston, Northamptonshire. His father, Mark Payne, was once Foreman for George Stephenson of locomotive fame, and it was at his father's steam-engine works that Walter served his apprenticeship. In 1882, at the age of 19, he moved to Coventry and soon found employment as a 'moulder' at Willdig & Hatton's, Brass Founders on Hales Street. It was whilst here that he became friends with a Mr Jack Bates, the son of a pub landlord who ran the Wheatsheaf Inn at Foleshill. Walter began to frequent this pub and became friendly with one of Jack's sisters, Harriet, who worked behind the bar. Before long they were married,

Walter Payne and Henry Bates pose in their Godiva car – the name also given to their motor-bicycle. (Coventry Transport Museum)

and Walter went to briefly work for Arthur Bonnick at the Bonnick Cycle Co. Meanwhile, Harriet's uncle, George Bates (born 1847), had just completed the sale of his hotel in London. With the profits he offered to set Walter on his way in business as an engine maker. Terms were agreed and new works were constructed for him at Godiva Street by 1890, establishing the Godiva Engineering Co. Joined by his older brothers, George and Frederick Payne, it was here that Walter is said to have developed the first petrol engine in the city in 1895. George Bates by now took a silent interest yet remained the majority shareholder, but his son Henry Bates (b. 1869) kept him informed of developments as he began to work more closely alongside the Payne brothers. By 1898 business was booming, and George Bates had a house built for Payne and his growing family on the Foleshill Road for them to rent. The house was quite impressive, complete with servant's quarters, and was constructed by builders John and Edmond Broad of Coventry, who had also built the works for Bates on Godiva Street and Foleshill Road. In 1900, the company began to build complete vehicles, including a motorcycle fitted with an AIV engine and also a car, both called the 'Godiva'. The company was also approached by Mr Charles Hamilton to build a car to his design, the result of which was called the 'Shamrock'. This was all cut short in 1901 when Payne's wife, Harriet, died from pneumonia, leaving him to raise six children. Disaster struck again shortly after with the death of George Bates. It was reported that in the winter of 1901 Henry Bates took his father and a 'Daimler employee' out for a test drive in one of the latest P&B cars. Taking a corner too fast, George was thrown from the vehicle and tragically died as a result of the injuries he sustained. As consequence of this, the Bates family sold all related assets, including the Godiva Street Works and the house on Foleshill Road, leaving Payne effectively unemployed and homeless. Fortunately, Payne and his brothers did own some small works built behind the Wheatsheaf Inn and at first rented them out, before selling them and re-establishing themselves at Castle Street by 1902. From here on in Payne seems to have recovered quite well as he was said to have continued building and supplying engines until his death in 1934. Both Walter Payne and George Bates are buried on the same plot near the gatehouse at St Paul's cemetery in Holbrooks, Coventry.

(See also Hamilton.)

GORTON, 1901 (1890–1901)

The Gorton Cycle & Motor Co., 36 Moor Street, Earlsdon

The origins of this company go back to 1890, when Wolverhampton brothers, Samuel and Bernard Gorton established Gorton, S&B Ltd at Whitefriars Cycle Works, Whitefriars Lane, Coventry. A year later, they also started another cycle company, the Quinton Cycle Co. at Quinton Road and Hertford Street. After almost ten years of cycle manufacture, the brothers appear to have gone their separate ways. Bernard joined Birmingham-born Thomas

The Gorton brothers first began making cycles in Coventry in 1890. (Coventry Transport Museum)

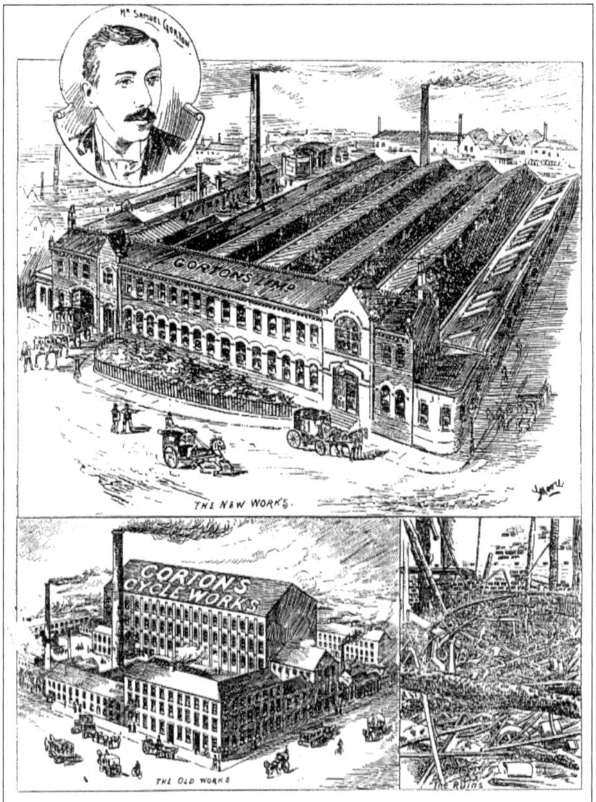

S. & B. GORTON, Ltd., QUINTON WORKS, COVENTRY.

Yardley and established the cycle firm of Gorton & Yardley Ltd at London Road. Meanwhile, Samuel Gorton was joined by son Edward A. Gorton, founding the Gorton Cycle & Motor Co. at Moor Street in Earlsdon. Here they began experimenting with fitting early motors to their own frames. This did not last long though, as shortly afterwards Samuel Gorton became Managing Director for the New Beeston Cycle Co., presumably a far more attractive offer. Whether Edward Gorton followed suit is unclear, but the 1901 census does list him as working in Coventry as a 'Cycle Motor Manufacturer'.
(See also Beeston.)

GRINDLAY-PEERLESS, 1923–1939 (1910–1986)

Grindlay (Coventry) Ltd, Melbourne Works & Shakleton Road, Spon End

Alfred Robert Grindlay was born in Coventry in 1876, and on leaving school at a young age, found work in one of the city's many cycle companies. The 1901 census shows him to be working as a 'Frame Builder at a Cycle Works' at the age of 25. This was for the Riley Cycle Co. where he worked directly under Allan Riley, and by 1909, Grindlay had worked his way up through the ranks to become Works Manager at the King Street factory. The following year, after some twenty years of experience, he decided to work for himself, setting up the Coventry Motor & Sundries Co. at Spon End, specialising in body-building. By 1921 he expanded his business interests and in partnership with Thomas E. Musson, started up another company as Musson & Grindlay, specialist sidecar makers.

These sidecars became very reputable, and this is supported by the fact that the company is known to have regularly exhibited them at the annual International Cycle, Motorcycle and Accessories Exhibition at Olympia in London, promoting them as 'sidecars to fit Triumph, Bradbury and Harley Davidson'. Two years later, in 1923, he

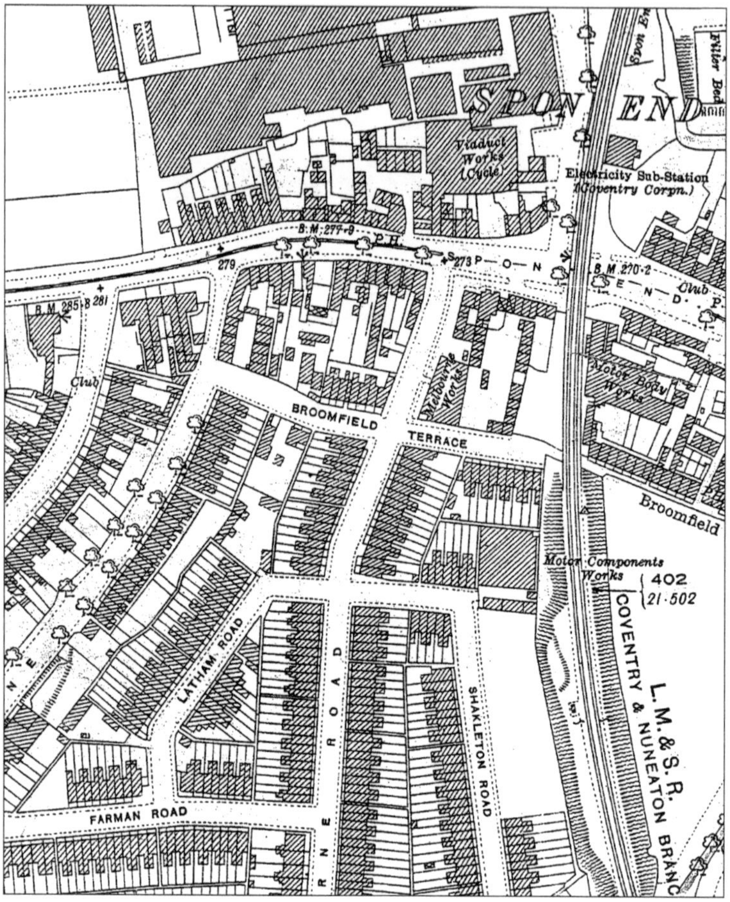

The Grindlay-Peerless factory was well hidden amongst the Spon End suburbs. It was positioned where the Motor Components Works can be seen here. (Ordnance Survey)

registered another company – that of Grindlay-Peerless, the latter part having the definition of having no equal or unrivaled. This new company had an interest in motorcycles of high power, their first offering being fitted with a 999cc sleeve-valve Barr & Stroud V-Twin engine. The next few years saw them experiment with many JAP and Barr & Stroud engines ranging from 344 to 499 in cubic capacity. Alfred's son Reginald Robert Grindlay had joined the firm as a young apprentice after the war. Known as 'Whiggy', he was a trials rider of some note, and was often seen around the Spon End Works wearing 'riding breeches, golf hose, tweed jacket and a scarf'.

The firm had been active on the competition circuit, notably Brooklands, and by 1926 they began to be fully acknowledged when their works rider Bill Lacey started winning regularly on his Grindlay-Peerless 344cc-powered JAP. Surely the company's greatest achievements came about in 1928 when Lacey set a 500cc world record by covering 100 miles in an hour (103.3 miles), something they repeated the following year (105.25 miles). At this time their road-production machines were being marketed as 'Built of the best and always ahead', whilst offering a replica 498cc machine to that which broke the one-hour world record for £90. As much as their race successes increased sales, it was a costly business, so in 1939 Grindlay and Peerless parted company. This was not the end of Grindlay though. To add to his Coventry Motor & Sundries firm, which was still going strong, he quickly registered yet another business called the Coventry Engineering Co., and was joined by sons Reginald and A.S.C. Grindlay. During the war, in 1941, Alfred Robert Grindlay was appointed Mayor of Coventry, and he was known to have taken out a number of motor related patents throughout the course of his long

Bill Lacey gained numerous victories on Grindlay-Peerless machines during the 1920s and '30s. (Coventry Transport Museum)

and successful career. His Coventry Engineering Co. was later listed in the Directory of Coventry Manufacturers of 1950 with Alfred as Director (C.B.E, J.P), and lists them as, 'specialising in jigs, fixtures, gauges, plastic moulds and press tools'. It is not clear when this firm eventually dissolved, but Coventry Motor Sundries Ltd was still in existence in 1986, with a Mr John Grindlay listed as Chairman.
(See also Riley.)

GSD, 1921–1923 (1921–1934)

GSD Motors Ltd, Smithford Street, 7 Arden Street & Canley Road

In 1921, Mr Reginald E.D. Grant, a resident of St Paul's Road, Coventry, established the firm of GSD Motors Ltd at Smithford Street, offering GSD motorcycles. The GSD stood for Grant Shaft-Drive, as developed by Grant himself after obtaining a BSc in Enginee.ring at Birmingham. The machines were available either with a 350cc two-stroke White & Poppe engine, or the larger 976cc JAP V-Twin model, and were first launched at the 1922 Olympia Motor Cycle Show in London. GSD's sales catalogue at the time confidentially stated: 'the only British Motorcycle with car refinements throughout at £85'. Grant obviously found it both difficult and expensive to break into such a market, so moved premises to Arden Street in Earlsdon, setting himself up as a 'Motor Engineer'. A final move followed to Canley Road, which is where Grant stayed until closure in 1934.

The GSD lightweight was on sale for just two years only from 1921. (Coventry Transport Museum)

Charles Hamilton (right) with his brother Willie in Coventry. (Sara J. Robinson)

HAMILTON, 1901–1907 (1901–1910)

Hamilton Motor Co., Priory Works, Dale Street

Charles Alexander Hamilton was born in Gortin, County Tyrone, Northern Ireland in 1874. In the early 1890s he moved to London where he studied engineering at Finsbury College, and it was during his years here that he became close friends with Charles Rolls, later of Rolls-Royce fame. By 1897 Hamilton had moved to Coventry working for the Daimler Co., and by 1901 had set up the Hamilton Motor Co. at Dale Street. Financed by two friends in Londonderry, Northern Ireland, Dr Todd and Mr H. Taaffe, Hamilton designed a car called the 'Shamrock'. This car was then constructed by Payne & Bates of Godiva Street, being a 20hp Phaeton-type machine with a water-cooled four-cylinder engine and three forward speeds. It was said to be capable of 35mph and was reported to be the first vehicle in Britain to use electrical sparking plugs. Before long, the Shamrock was exhibited at the first motor exhibition at the Agricultural Show in London. In 1901, Hamilton himself drove his family down to London in this car for Queen Victoria's funeral. At around the same time some more influential friends of Hamilton, Colonel Sir William F. Wyley and a Dr Phillips, again financed him, this time to make motorcycles in his Dale Street premises. These were powered by 2¼hp, 3¼hp, 4hp and 4½hp engines, the latter being a V-Twin model and built until 1907. In 1908, Hamilton married Edith Jane Burrell at St Paul's Church, Foleshill. After 1910, he went on to work for Humber, and later, Rover, working under Peter Poppe. He completed his working life back at the Daimler Co. until retirement, and after spending many years residing at Moseley Avenue, Hamilton died in 1956 and is rested at Canley Crematorium, Coventry.
(See also Godiva.)

HAMMON & SMITH

(See Clarendon.)

The Hamilton Motor Co. was established in 1901. (Sara J. Robinson)

A rare glimpse of a Hamilton motor-bicycle. (Vintage Motor Cycle Club)

Hamilton worked at the Daimler Co. towards the end of his productive career. (Sara J. Robinson)

HAZLEWOODS, 1911–1927 (1876–1927)

Hazlewood's Ltd, Albion Mills, 52 West Orchard

New Hazlewood Cycle Co. Ltd, 21 Upper Well Street

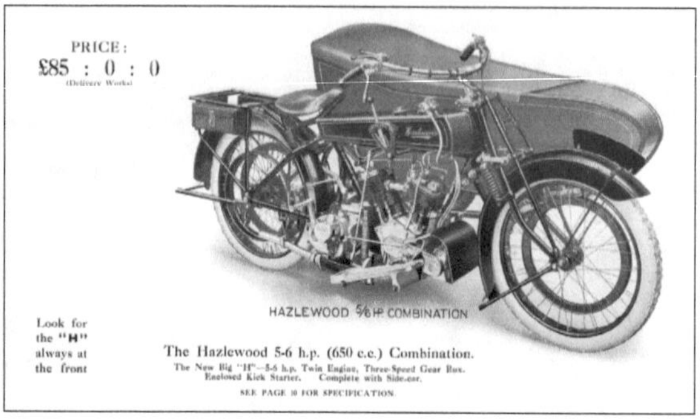

A Hazlewood combination offered from £85. (Coventry Transport Museum)

Hazlewood's Ltd had a very long history in cycle making before they too embarked on motorcycle production in 1911. They were established in 1876 at Albion Mills, West Orchard, an address that although still exists in the city, now takes on a completely different appearance as a shopping mall. It's founders can be narrowed down to three men on looking at the 1901 census: James Hazlewood, born 1838 in Banbury, working in Coventry as a 'Cycle Manufacturer'; his son, also James Hazlewood, born 1860 in Banbury and working in Coventry as a 'Cycle Manufacturer', and William Hazlewood, born 1867 in Knightcote, Warwickshire, again working in Coventry as a 'Cycle Manufacturer'. It is very probable that William is also James' son, born after the family moved from Oxfordshire to the Coventry area sometime between 1860 and 1867. After some twenty-nine years of pure cycle making, the company began to make sidecars. For some reason they did not enter the motorcycle market until 1911, with their first machines being powered by 2¾hp JAP engines, increased to 5hp by 1913, and exhibited at the International Cycle, Motorcycle & Accessories Show in London the same year. They continued production throughout the war and by 1920 offered a 654cc V-Twin model, and the following year, a 976cc version. By the 1922 season, their sales catalogue for cycles and motorcycles stated, 'Always look for the big "H" on the front' – a feature that was clearly visible on their models. By 1926/27 they had reformed as the New Hazlewood Cycle Co., and based at 21 Upper Well Street. At this point they were still listed as 'Cycle and Motorcycle Manufacturers' but nothing is known about Hazlewood's from then on.

HILLMAN, 1902

Hillman Motor Co., South Street, Hood Street & Humber Road

William Hillman was born on 30 December 1847 at Lewisham, Kent. After studying engineering at Penn's Ship Engine Builders in Greenwich, London, he came to Coventry in the mid-1860s, finding employment at the Coventry Machinists Co. under the wings of James Starley and Josiah Turner. It was here that Hillman became involved in the new cycle industry and where he really began to apply his engineering skills. In November 1873, he married Fanny Moreton Brockas and by 1875 he formed the Hillman & Herbert Cycle Co. together with W.H. Herbert at the Premier Bicycle & Tricycle Works. In 1880, they teamed up with George Cooper to form Hillman, Herbert & Cooper Ltd at South Street. By now, Hillman's business interests were booming with the addition of a new venture, the Sparkbrook Cycle Co., and this can be measured by the fact that his growing family are seen to be moving up in society, buying a house known as Stoke Road Villa in the leafy Stoke area of the city.

Above: Hillman produced his own motor-bicycle in 1902, but chose not to develop the end result. (Coventry Transport Museum)

Right: William Hillman made his fortune through the sales of cycles and motorised transport in Coventry. (Coventry Transport Museum)

The 1890s witnessed much experimentation with motor-driven vehicles in Coventry and many of the cycle companies quickly got involved. Hillman was no different, and in 1902 he developed an all-chain-driven motor-bicycle fitted with a 1½hp engine, using a float chamber and magneto ignition. The frame was said to be quite unusual, as was the engine position, mounted behind the headstock, at the front of the frame. The complete machine was extremely well made and very advanced, yet for some reason the company did not pursue the idea, and focused instead on cycle making. In 1907 Hillman returned to motoring when he teamed up with Louis Coatalen to form the Hillman-Coatalen Motor Co. at Hood Street, and by 1910 the Hillman Motor Co. at Humber Road, which was to prove an enormous success. Two of his six daughters later married significant men in the Coventry motor industry, these being Captain John Black (MD of Standard Triumph and formerly Hillman as Sales Manager), and Spencer Bernau Wilks (MD of Rover). William Hillman died in February 1921 at his Keresley Hall home, and is buried nearby at St Thomas' Church on Tamworth Road, Coventry.
(See also Premier, and Sparkbrook.)

HOBART, 1901–1923 (1892–1934)

Hobart, Bird & Co. Ltd, Hobart Motor Works, 287–295 Stoney Stanton Road, Bishopsgate Green, & 55 St Patrick's Road, Cheylesmore
Hobart Cycle Co. Ltd, St Patrick's Road, Cheylesmore

The Hobart name is yet another that originates back to cycle making. Hobart, Bird & Co. were thought to have been founded in Wolverhampton around 1892, but by 1897 they are seen to be operating out of a factory at St Patrick's Road, Cheylesmore, Coventry. At this time, Wolverhampton and Birmingham were also very active in cycle manufacture, so the reason why the company moved to Coventry is unclear. Two possibilities so far exist that may unearth the identities of the person or people who founded this cycle company. The 1901 census does not reveal anyone by the Hobart name in the Midlands connected to the cycle industry, yet there is an Alfred F. Bird aged 51 of Birmingham, working in Birmingham as a 'Cycle Manufacturer'. It could be plausible then that Mr Hobart either left or died between 1892 and 1897, and the company was sold by Mr Bird to new owners who either moved to,

A Hobart motorcycle of 1913. Records of the company's founders remains somewhat unclear. (Mortons Media)

A beautifully constructed Hobart ladies model of 1912. (Mortons Media)

or already lived in Coventry, with Bird then starting up a new cycle business under a separate name in Birmingham. Another strong possibility is that of a Mr William Hobart Bird, who can be seen working as an Ironmonger in Coventry from 1877. An advertisment by the company in the 1911 *Bicycling News & Motor Review* adds to the confusion by stating that 'more than fifty thousand cycles and motorcycles have been built in our factory since we began business in 1884 – Hobart, Bird & Co., Ltd Coventry'. Nevertheless, as well as building cycles, in 1901 Hobart, Bird & Co. began to experiment with motors, fitting inclined engines to frames. As developments progressed they began building machines complete with vertical 2½hp Dalton & Wade engines. According to the November 1902 edition of the *Motor-Car Journal* they exhibited a specially designed motor-bicycle at the Stanley Show that year. According to Harold Connolly in his 1962 book *Motorcycle Story*, 'the Hobart Co. had a reputation for building very well finished bicycles, and the same high workmanship was apparent in their motorcycles. They were one of the earliest firms to use a large size tyre, which added very greatly to the comfort of the rider. The engine was 2¼hp with an automatic inlet-valve and a loop frame was used'. As well as developing their 'Handy Hobart' motorcycle they also supplied frames and engines to other firms. They were also consistent on the racing stage, gaining a 100-mile record at Brooklands in 1911, and still competing ten years later, including a machine entered at the 1921 Brooklands 500-mile race, ridden by G.G. Savage, who finished third in the 250cc class. *(See also McKenzie, and Hobart-Acme.)*

George Ravenhall in action at the Isle of Man TT in 1921. (Ron Ravenhall)

HOBART-ACME, 1923–1924

Hobart-Acme Motors Ltd, Cheylesmore Works, St Patrick's Road & Osborne Road, Earlsdon

After some forty years in the cycle and motor industry, the Hobart Co. ran into difficulties and in 1923 were taken over by Coventry-based Rex-Acme, forming a new company known as Hobart-Acme Motors Ltd. The 1924 Kelly's Warwickshire Directory lists them under 'Motorcycle Manufacturers' as 'Hobart-Acme Motors Ltd, Cheylesmore Works, St Patrick's Road'. Rex-Acme obviously saw this takeover as being an investment for their own future production, most probably with the new Hobart concern taking care of the engine side of things. They did, however produce a motorcycle under the Hobart-Acme name, in addition to the Rex-Acme machines in the hope of generating further interest. Unfortunately it wasn't to be, and within a year Hobart-Acme was no more. The Rex side did survive though, continuing to produce motorcycles until it was bought by the sidecar makers, Mills-Fulford in 1932.

(See also Hobart, and Rex-Acme.)

H&R, 1923 (1922–1925)

Ravenhall & Hailstone, 132 Clay Lane, Stoke

For some reason, the company of Ravenhall & Hailstone sold their motorcycle under the R&H name, but also under the H&R marque for 1923. But apart from the change of name, the machine itself was basically the same – a 147cc Villiers lightweight with a two-speed Albion gearbox. They sold the R&H version until closure in 1925, which saw both men go separate ways.

(See also R&H)

HUBBARD, 1904–1905 (1889–1913)

Hubbard Motor & Engineering Co., Much Park Street

The man responsible for starting the Hubbard Motor & Engineering Co. was William Hubbard. On finishing his education, he first worked on a lathe at Joseph Jessop's engineering company at Leicester. In 1889 he formed an early partnership with his old school friend, Alfred Herbert, both buying the company of Coles & Matthews at the Butts, Coventry for £4,000

An early Hubbard forecar. William Hubbard established both the Hubbard and Whitley businesses in Coventry. (Vintage Motor Cycle Club)

and renaming the firm Herbert & Hubbard. In their book *Life & Labour in a Twentieth Century City*, Lancaster and Mason state, 'with Hubbard's considerable inventive capacity they began making drilling machines, rim bending machines, spoke screwing machines, and hand lathe's, which sold freely at about £28 a piece'. Although the business was doing very well, the two men had differing opinions about the future direction of the business. In the end, Herbert bought out Hubbard's share and they parted company. Alfred Herbert went on to make a massive name for himself in the machine tool industry, with Hubbard turning his attention to motorised transport. In 1902 he set up the Whitley Motor Co. at Cow Lane, building 'Whitley' engines, motor-bicycles and forecars. Two years later he established a second company under the Hubbard name, where he developed a forecar and motor-bicycle fitted with a 4½hp water-cooled engine compete with two-speed gears and flat-belt final drive. By 1905, the Hubbard concern appears to end, yet William Hubbard himself continued with the Whitley Motor Co. until at least 1910. In 1912/13, however, Hubbard & Sons Ltd, a cycle company, was based at Queen Victoria Road, Coventry, which may be connected.
(See also Whitley.)

HUMBER, 1896–1933 (1868–1968)

Humber & Co. Ltd, Lower Ford Street, Hillfields
Humber Ltd, Humber Works, Humber Road, Stoke

In transport terms, the name of Humber is one that spans a century and stretches from the beginnings of the cycle industry to the peak of the British motor industry. It is also a name connected with one of the very first motorcycles to be built in Britain. Thomas Humber was born in 1841 in Sheffield. He moved to Nottingham in 1854 becoming an Apprentice Wheelwright and Blacksmith for William Campion. With an interest in road transport he kept an eye on the development of the cycle, and in 1868, is said to have built his first velocipede. In 1874 he was joined by Thomas Rushforth Marriott and Frederick Cooper, forming Humber, Marriott & Cooper as Cycle Manufacturers. In 1878 they moved to a new factory at Beeston, Nottinghamshire – Humber was said to be the engineer, Marriott the businessman, and Cooper

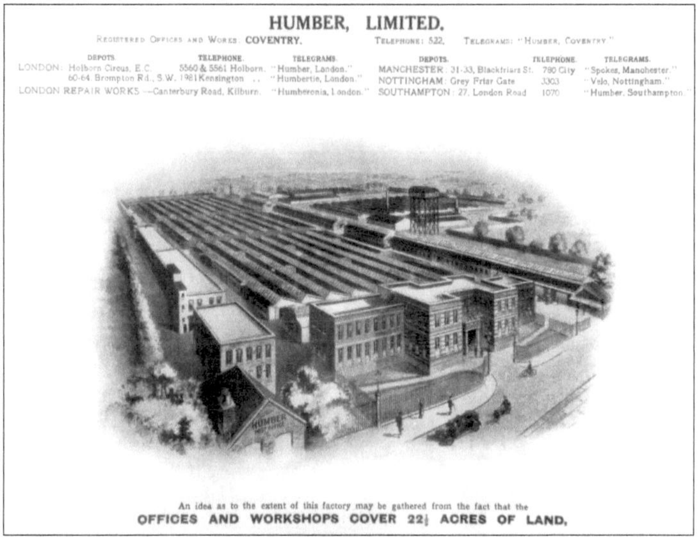

The Humber Co.'s 'new' works of 1908. (Coventry Transport Museum)

Humber's finishing shop with Bert Yates pictured far right. (Coventry Transport Museum)

A Humber lightweight machine of the 1920s. (Coventry Transport Museum)

the racer. In 1885, Humber opened up a second cycle factory in Coventry, first at Whitefriars Lane, and the following year at Lower Ford Street as Humber & Co. Ltd. The Lower Ford Street site was in fact the former home of cycle builders, Townend Brothers, and was extensively enlarged by Humber. In 1896, when Humber first began engaging in motorised transport, the factory was destroyed by fire. Also destroyed was a primitive vehicle built by Wolfmuller & Geisenhof in Paris that the company had purchased to study its working mechanics. Harry J. Lawson and Ernest Hooley then bought an interest in Humber as it went out of private ownership, and by doing so acquired their workforce, providing them with adequate additional space to use at the newly acquired 'Motor Mills'. With Walter Phillips and Alexander Craig as Works Managers, Lawson got the Humber team involved in many early motoring projects including developing Kane-Pennington designs and also British-built versions of the Leon Bollee machines called the 'Coventry Motette'. *The Autocar* of June 1896 wrote, 'The first practical motor cycle built in this country was completed last week when Humber & Co. finished a bicycle fitted with a Pennington 2hp motor made at their works in Coventry'. In 1898, Humber also produced an electric tandem known as the 'Olympia' based on a Pennington design that was used for cycle pacing on cycle tracks. It was not until 1902 that Humber made a more serious approach to motorcycle production with a belt-driven model powered by a 1½hp engine hung from the downtube. It was around the same time that the company had began to adopt Phelon & Rayner designs under license and became forerunners in powered racing competitions, with works rider Bert Yates at the helm. From 1903, Humber's manufacturing in Coventry was limited due to accommodation difficulties and much motorised development transferred to the company's factory at Beeston while new modern works were being developed at Coventry. By 1908, a large proportion of production moved back to Coventry at the new Humber Road site in the Stoke area, employing around 5,000 men. By this time Humber were concentrating more heavily on car production, yet still developed cycles and motorcycles to a lesser extent. Up to the outbreak of war, they offered a range of machines from 2hp upwards and were ever-present on the racing circuit. Post-war saw the introduction of a 'Sports' road model as well as a 349cc sv single by 1923, but slowly the car took preference, seeing all motorcycle production phased out in 1933.
(See also Centaur, Lawson, and Phelon-Humber.)

Bert Yates (1869–1923)

The name of Bert Yates is one that is now rarely remembered in the motorcycle world, yet from the late 1890s until the outbreak of the First World War he was very well known and respected on the national trials and racing circuits.

Egbert Yates was born on 29 January 1869 at Clee Hills, Shropshire, one of the most mountainous parts of the Midlands. He started cycling at the age of 14, which began his passion for racing.

After first finding work as a Machinist, in the 1890s he moved to Wren Street, in the Hillfields area of Coventry and found employment at the nearby Humber Motor Co. He married a woman by the name of Ruth Francis of Leamington and together they had three children. Humber had established a base in Coventry in 1885 as cycle manufacturers, but was one of the first companies in the country specialising in motor production.

Being one of the first men in Coventry to be at the forefront of motor development, Yates spoke of these early motoring times in his later years:

> My first introduction to the motor cycle (a monstrosity never again equalled to this day, but on several occasions run pretty close) was in the year 1895. This machine was designed by an American, 'Pennington' by name. I will pass over the troubles and trials this machine was heir to. It lived, and died, and, in its dying brought to life others which were in turn stepping stones to the beautiful machines we see on the road today.

Bert Yates poses for a promotional shot in his Humber racing gear. (Leon Tavinor)

Bert Yates was reported to have been the first man in Great Britain to win a staged motorcycle race. (Leon Tavinor)

In 1896, Humber had developed their own motorcycle, and before too long, they and other newly formed companies began racing their machines against one another. Bert Yates soon rose to become Department Head Engineer and a gifted works rider for Humber, and was active right at the very beginnings of motorised racing. He can in fact proudly lay claim to being a competitor in the first motorcycle race to be held in Britain, and ultimately winning. This historic event was staged at the Butts Cycle Track, Coventry on 10 July 1899.

From this proud first victory, Yates then concentrated on developing the machines themselves at Humber, before returning to competitive racing more seriously in 1902, when he won no less than sixteen races in that year. Notable successes included the Starley Challenge Cup, the Automobile Club's 650-miles trial, and the 5-mile handicap at Villa Park. The years 1903 and 1905 saw a further nineteen victories before Yates took another break from racing, this time a lengthier one.

Due to accommodation issues, Humber decided to halt the production of motorcycles late in 1906 while they concentrated on producing cars. At this time, Bert and his family decided to uproot to Canada, where one of his jobs was, reportedly, riding the 'Wall of Death' in front of large crowds. It was not until after the Humber Co. had moved to new extended works in the Stoke area of Coventry that in 1909 the Yates family returned home. Motorcycle production at this point resumed and Yates once more returned to racing.

With the exception of the 1912 season, Yates was virtually ever-present for Humber in competitions. He also became Coventry's Motorcycle Club Captain. In 1910, he was one of five Humber entrants at the Isle of Man TT, along with John F. Crundall, F.G. Edmonds, D.M. Brown and Sam Wright, but all without success. In July of that year, however, Yates took the Gold Medal at the ACU Land's End to John O'Groats event, and later, first place at Kendal.

In the years 1911 and 1913, he gained worthy successes at Brooklands. In 1911 he took both the 1-Hour Record and the 50-Mile Record on a 2hp Humber, and in 1913, won the 350cc three-lap scratch race. By 1914, at the age of 45, he bowed out of competitive racing after one final project, being racing mechanic to Sam Wright.

His early experiences of motorised transport make for interesting reading at a time when we have now advanced so far in the industry that reliability, safety and comfort are taken for granted. The following account describes testing Humber motorcycles around the Coventry area:

Bert Yates, pictured with his wife and family outside their home, *c.* 1910. (Leon Tavinor)

Bert Yates and wife Ruth seated at a racing event, *c.* 1900. (Leon Tavinor)

> One afternoon, somewhere in England, I decided to give the machine a thorough test, a more extended one than I had ever dared attempt hitherto. After getting my lamp ignition to burn in a reasonable state of efficiency I let her rip. All went well till I had covered some 20 miles, without a stop, which by the way created an unofficial record for such prehistoric days. Suddenly without any warning, something flashed by me, and before I could realise what it was, I thought all the devils incarnate had been let loose; I looped the loop, whirled the whirl, and finished up by going head first into a pool of dirty mud and water. I managed eventually to extricate myself, and having regained my normal eyesight, and having found nothing broken except my pipe, I started to find out what all the fuss was about. Still remembering the flash that had passed me, I started hunting for the bike, this I found firmly fixed in a hedge a few yards away. On examination, I found the flywheel had come adrift and was missing, which naturally accounted for the flash that had gone by. The trouble solved, the problem now was to find the flywheel, but quite as important the nut and washer that held this in position; these I found very soon lying side by side not a dozen yards from the place of the accident; having found these, my load of trouble seemed to lighten. I commenced quite casually to look for the flywheel, little thinking that a mass of metal like this could escape observation; dear readers it escaped MY observation, for five solid weary hours; dragging ditches, poking in and pulling down hedges was my occupation for the rest of the afternoon, but no flywheel could I find. At length, giving up in disgust I sat on a gate. I don't know why I did this, but I did, thinking, wondering, and at the same time little realising that in a few years time, snorting 'Indians', 'Triumphs' and 'Norton's' would be dashing by. Years have passed since then, and I can now picture myself sitting there viewing the ghosts of the future. I also began to wonder how home was to be reached, when low and behold, jammed between the second and third bars of the gate I was sitting on, rested the flywheel, its plated rim glistening in the moonlight. It had jumped or rather flown (thereby proving its existence and name) from the road, into this unheard of position. You will imagine my feelings better than my pen can describe them. However, I soon had this trouble fixed, to find still more. The front tyre was punctured. It was no light task to mend a puncture then. Still this was overcome, and like the beetle I started wending homeward my droning flight.

Bert Yates final years were spent in Leamington Spa, where he worked as Foreman in the machine shop at Flavells. He died in 1923 at the age of 54 and is buried at St Mary Magdalene's Church, Lillington. His astounding successes in racing came at a time when safety was minimal and dangers ever-present. Lessons were often learned the hard way, yet as a result, pioneers such as Yates paved the way for improved engineering methods and ultimately greater motorcycles from then on.

INVICTA, 1912–1926 (1902–1926)
A. Barnett & Co., 58 West Orchard & Lloyds Bank Chambers, High Street

Arthur Barnett was born in Coventry in 1863. On finishing his education he worked for one of the city's smaller cycle manufacturers in accounts, before obtaining a higher profile job at the massive Singer Co. The 1901 census supports this and shows Barnett as working as a 'Cashier in the Cycle Trade'. He steadily worked his way up in the company and eventually became a Director, but by 1912 he took the decision to form his own business. On acquiring premises at West Orchard and the High Street, he established A. Barnett & Co., building cycles and motorcycles called the 'Invicta', the Latin name meaning 'unconquerable'. These machines were built using 269cc two-stroke Villiers, 678cc JAP and 499cc Abingdon engines, mostly sold for the export market. In 1919 he part-formed the company of Francis-Barnett at Lower Ford Street with son-in-law, Gordon Francis. Although now marketing Francis-Barnett machines they continued to offer the Invicta marque for a few more years. In 1922, they entered an Invicta lightweight model at the Isle of Man TT ridden by J. Joynson, but unfortunately it

An Invicta TT model of 1915. (Mortons Media)

A rare photograph of an Invicta motorcycle with owner. (Coventry Transport Museum)

failed to complete the course. By 1926 Francis and Barnett dropped the Invicta name and concentrated on developing their own motorcycles, which remained in production until 1964. *(See also Francis-Barnett.)*

JOHNSON, HURLEY & MARTIN

(See Alpha.)

JOHNSON-TYLER, 1924–1927

Johnson, Tyler & Co., 15 Chapel Street

This company entered the motorcycle market in 1924, with a two-stroke twin-cylinder model. Ex-Triumph employees Johnson and Tyler were most probably a firm of mechanical engineers initially with a specialist interest in motorcycles. Soon they were listed as 'Motorcycle Manufacturers and General Dealers', building their own machines from parts supplied from elsewhere. Their workshop was situated in Chapel Street, a very old central street now occupied by post-war developments. Johnson, Tyler & Co. made a final listing in the Coventry Spennell Directory of 1926/27, but nothing was seen of them after this date.

JONES, 1911–1913 (1911–1936)

E. Gilbert Jones, 10 Garden Row, 24 Smithford Street

Gilbert Jones was just 16 when he moved to Coventry from Dublin around 1900. He quickly gained employment in the cycle industry and after ten years experience, decided to go it alone. In 1911 he established a business in a courtyard off Smithford Street, locally known as 'Garden Row', and can be seen in the Kelly's Directory of that year listed as a 'Motorcycle Manufacturer and Motor Engineer'. The full details of the Jones motorcycle are not known, but it would appear that it was a short-lived affair, as by 1919 he is listed only under 'Engineers'. However, Jones must have been a reputable motor engineer, as he was known to have still been trading at Smithford Street until around 1936.

JONES, 1924–1927 (1897–1929)

W.M. Jones, Empire Works, 37 Clarendon Street, Earlsdon

Like the previous Jones marque, little is known about the specific details surrounding this motorcycle. Yet the 1924 Kelly's Directory clearly shows a Mr W.M. Jones listed as a 'Motorcycle Manufacturer' at the Empire Works at Clarendon Street, Earlsdon. It is thought that Jones began the Caesar Cycle Co. in 1897, offering two-year guarantees on his products. By 1919 he is seen to be primarily working as a 'Cycle and Motor Exporter' of his Caesar machines and other motors. In 1923 he was offering Caesar motorcycles, powered by 269cc Villiers engines, yet the following year began marketing them under the 'Jones' name. By 1927 he is still listed as a 'Motorcycle Manufacturer' but also as supplying components for the trade. Nothing is seen of him in Coventry after 1929.

(See also Caesar.)

KENILWORTH, 1919–1924

Booth Bros., Bishop Street & Lamb Street
Kenilworth Utility Motors Ltd, Much Park Street

This machine was the brainchild of Captain George Thomas Smith-Clarke after the First World War. Smith-Clarke was born in Bewdley, Worcestershire in 1884 and began his working life as a bus conductor in the Midlands, which supported his academic studies. As early as 1900 he had developed a tricycle, and in 1904, a motorcycle made of water piping powered by a Clement-Garrard engine. He then found employment for the Great Western Railway and by 1913 had risen to Chief Draughtsman at the Royal Motor Department at Slough. Two years later, he gained the rank of Captain, as Officer in Charge (Engines) Aeronautical Inspection Directorate for Coventry. He was soon responsible for the inspection of 19,000 aero engines built in Coventry during the war. Smith-Clarke was then appointed Assistant Works Manager at Daimler until 1922 when he joined the Alvis Motor Co. as Chief Engineer. In 1919 the Kenilworth design prototype was taken up initially by Kenilworth Utility Motors, and then the Booth Brothers, commencing production at their Bishop Street Works in Coventry. The machine was originally made for his wife and called the G.S.C. Autocyclette. It was built using a fully sprung open-frame of triangulated tubes, powered by 143cc Norman, 269cc Villiers and 292cc JAP engines until 1924.

George Smith-Clarke pictured (right) during his Alvis days in 1925. (Coventry Transport Museum)

KINGSWAY, 1920–1922

Kingsway Motor Cycle Co., 44 Brighton Street, Stoke

Nothing is known about the men who founded the Kingsway Motorcycle Co., except that in 1920 they began production of lightweight machines fitted with a two-stroke 269cc Arden, and sleeve-valve JAP engines from £55. They worked out of a small unit in Brighton Street in the Stoke area of the city, most probably in the backyard of the house itself. Brighton Street is actually a continuation of a street known as 'Kingsway' in Stoke, and obviously from which the owners took their company name. Considering that the war had not long concluded, it was optimistic of Kingsway to think that they could break into a market already offering machines of similar design, which is more than likely why they ultimately closed in under two years.

LANCER, 1904–1905 (1901–1906)

Lancer Cycle & Motor Co., Coventry

This company began life as a cycle firm in 1901 at an unknown address in Coventry. By 1904 they had progressed to build motorised machines powered by locally built MMC, Minerva, and their own engines of 2hp, 2¾hp and 3½hp, but this was to last just under a year. The name Lancer does not reveal the identity of the person or people who founded the company from the 1901 census. That being, the name must have been chosen for its literal meaning, 'a cavalry man armed with a fighting spear'.

(See also MMC.)

Henry Lawson was paramount in developing Coventry as the hub of motor production. (Coventry Transport Museum)

Lawson purchased an old cotton factory in Coventry and transformed it into the famous 'Motor Mills'. (Coventry Transport Museum)

LAWSON, 1880 & 1900–1901

H.J. Lawson, Motor Mills, Sandy Lane, Bishopgate Green

Henry (or Harry) John Lawson is perhaps one of the most influential and significant men to have been involved in the British motor industry, yet for all his pioneering work it is unfortunate to discover that when he died in 1925, all he left was a reported £99 gross. An elusive character, Lawson was born in London in February 1852. His involvement in the British cycle industry began very early on. Having earned a two-year apprenticeship in engineering at W. Melville's Iron Factors at Islington, it was here that he built his first bicycle in the 'Boneshaker' mould. In 1873 his family moved to Brighton where he found employment with James Likeman, and together they developed what was reputed to be the first 'safety bicycle' in that year. Lawson left Brighton around 1878, and took up the position of Sales Manager at Haynes & Jefferis in Coventry. He then merged this firm into that of the Tangent & Coventry Tricycle Co. before starting up the Queen Cycle Co. at 860 Railway Buildings some time later. Lawson made a lot of money out of the cycle industry during these years, not only in his own concerns, but also in the promotion and marketing of other companies. In 1880 he was pivotal in transforming the Tangent concern into the Rudge Cycle Co. in association with Coventry solicitor, George Woodcock. Having patented designs for the first oil-driven car and compressed gas-powered motor-bicycle in England, also in 1880, Lawson naturally began to keep a very close eye on developments in motorised transport. In 1895, in conjunction with Ernest Terah Hooley, he approached Frederick Richard Simms who had recently bought the foreign patent rights of the petrol engine. Lawson offered Simms a large sum of money for the patents of which he duly accepted. Lawson then established the British Motor Syndicate with a capital of £150,000, acquiring many more patents along the way including Daimler, Werner, Bollee and De Dion Bouton, and by doing so, effectively founded the British motor industry. After viewing potential sites in other towns and cities, he finally opted for a large cotton mill in Coventry because of the city's already skilled and readily available workforce, renaming the building the 'Motor Mills'. This site soon became a hub of

Pennington machines were some of the first to be developed under Lawson's watchful eye at the 'Motor Mills'. (Coventry Transport Museum)

motoring activity as Lawson established Daimler as the country's first car manufacturer, along with other floated companies on other floors, including Humber, Pennington and the Great Horseless Carriage Co. In 1900 Lawson developed his own experimental motorised bicycle, with the engine mounted behind the rear wheel. This design was said to be similar to that which was simultaneously being developed by the American Edward Joel Pennington, who had befriended Lawson with his innovative ideas in transportation. Unfortunately, this association would play a costly part in Lawson's demise, when he paid Pennington the massive sum of £100,000 for his designs, which later proved to be complete fabrications. In May 1904, Lawson and fellow company promoter Ernest Terah Hooley were both arrested and charged with conspiracy to defraud. Lawson was personally sentenced to one year's hard labour, yet stated in court, 'if such business and connections have brought me to Bow Street, then I am proud of being there.'

(See also Accles, Beeston, Century, Coventry Motette, Humber, MMC, MSC, Pennington, Pennington-Sturmey, Phelon-Humber, and Werner.)

LEA-FRANCIS, 1911–1924 (1895–1960)

Lea & Francis Ltd, Lower Ford Street

Richard Henry Lea and Graham Inglesby Francis entered into partnership in August 1895 selling 'Lea' cycles at Day's Lane, Coventry. Lea was born on 23 February 1858, the son of a cabinet maker, and was raised in Lutterworth, Leicestershire. He was educated at Manchester Grammar School before joining Singer & Co. in 1878, staying with the firm until 1895 when he joined Francis. Whilst at Singer, Lea spent a lot of his time abroad drumming up sales in India, the Far East and America, until being appointed Works Manager at Singers 'New Works' in 1888. Francis also spent much time abroad in his early career. Born in London in 1862, he first found employment at the machine tool makers Ludwig, Loewe & Co., in

Don Francis (right) and works colleagues pose for a picture before embarking on an endurance race. (Coventry Transport Museum)

Berlin, before moving to America to take up employment, first with Brown & Sharpe, and then Pratt & Witney. After returning to England, he moved to Coventry in 1891, becoming General Manager of the Auto Machinery Co. This firm was formed by William Hillman (later of the Premier Co.) and George Sumner, and were specialists in ball bearings. By 1895 Lea and Francis had come together, initially setting up at Day's Lane. The following year they moved to more extensive works at Lower Ford Street, owned by Lord Leigh. James Stone was appointed the first Works Manager; John Rudd as Secretary, and F.A. Griffin became General Manager. The company quickly earned a solid reputation for producing high quality cycles, gaining many high-profile customers along the way including Lord Burleigh. By 1900 many of the other city cycle manufacturers had began experimenting with motorised transport, fitting engines to their frames. For some reason, Lea and Francis opted to bypass this and build a car instead, designed by the Scot, Alexander Craig. The finished article however, was not a success and severely tested the company's finances. It wasn't until 1911 that the first motorcycle was built for production. This was a lightweight machine fitted with a 3¼hp JAP V-Twin engine instigated by Richard Lea, his son Norman, Don Francis, Clifford Ingall and Marcus Nash, and priced at £68 5*s*. Continuing their fine reputation in cycle making, Lea and Francis' motorcycles were equally well received, one of their first customers being none other than George Bernard Shaw. Although Shaw was by now in his fifties, he had taken up motorcycling as a hobby. On purchasing his Lea-Francis motorcycle, he personally went to collect it in his chauffeur-driven car. He then instructed the driver to leave him and began riding his new machine down Lower Ford Street on route back to London. It is said that members of the Lea-Francis workforce reported that he was 'steering none-too-straight a course' as he travelled down the road. Even with a reduced workforce, the company produced motorcycles right through the war, but fell into difficulties during the early 1920s. After a series of price reductions the decision was made by the board to focus on producing motorcars. The remaining motorcycles were sold on to staff at discount prices.

(See also Francis-Barnett, and Hillman.)

Don Francis pictured on a finely crafted Lea-Francis machine. (Coventry Transport Museum)

Clifford Ingall makes some roadside adjustments to his Lea-Francis. (Coventry Transport Museum)

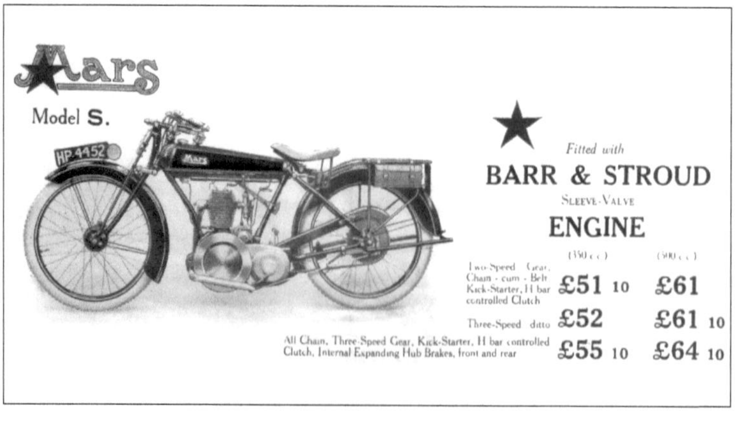

Mars motorcycles were fitted with various engines supplied by the most reputable of companies. (Coventry Transport Museum)

MARS, 1922–1926

Mars Ltd, Whitefriar's Lane

With a name taken from the God of War, the Mars Co. began life in 1922 at an address in Whitefriar's Lane, an ancient Coventry Street. Thought to have been under the control of former Premier Company Manager Peter Moss (b. 1881), Mars began using various capacity two-stroke Villiers, JAP, oil-cooled Bradshaw and sleeve-valve Barr & Stroud engines, fitted to frames of their own manufacture. All models were built using modern saddle tanks by late 1923. Their emblem was a bold one, featuring a red star, and on their sales brochures the company confidently stated 'every machine perfect'. In 1924 they were offering four motorcycles ranging from £32 to £64. By the mid-1920s, large firms such as Triumph and Rudge were turning out thousands of motorcycles whilst bringing prices down. The likes of Mars could never compete with such giants, which is why they and many others ultimately failed in the market.

MARSEAL, 1920–1921 (1919–1925)

Marseal Engineering Co., Victoria Park, Harefield Road, Stoke

The Marseal Engineering Co. made a brief appearance in the motorcycle market in 1920. This took the form of an odd-looking scooter fitted with a 2hp 232cc two-stroke engine of minimal comfort and design. Unsurprisingly, few were ever made, but the brief history of the company is an interesting one. It was formed by the meeting of two men; Captain Donald Marcus Kelway Marendaz and Charles A. Seelhoff. Marendaz was born in Glamorgan, Wales in 1897 to a Swiss family, and Seelhoff, of Belgian descent, was born in 1893 in Staffordshire. Before the war, both had worked for the Coventry car company Siddeley-Deasy, and it was during their time here that they had decided to make a car of their own. The plans were put on hold though as both served their adoptive country during wartime, Marendaz being part of the RAF Royal Flying Corps no. 35 squadron and invalided back to England in 1918. When both had returned they first gained employment at the newly formed Alvis Co., specialising in gearboxes. Soon after, they found premises at Harefield Road in Stoke, Coventry, calling the new company Marseel – taken from the beginning of their two surnames. However, the partnership proved to be very shortlived when Seelhoff suddenly decided to pull out. Marendaz continued on, but changed the company name to 'Marseal' instead and developed a car of his own design. He raced this machine at Brooklands, but racing proved to be costly, and by 1925 the company folded. He then set up a new firm in Camberwell building cars that looked suspiciously like Bentleys. The Bentley Motor Co. caught wind of this and considered taking legal action, but backed down when they learned of Marendaz' poor financial position and decided his cars were of no real threat to them. He continued to race with marginal success in cars built by Graham-Paige until 1931. The following year he started another company at Maidenhead, but this collapsed in 1936. He then moved to Bedford and started a flying school before establishing Marendaz Aircraft Ltd, building bi-planes. He had become progressively active in politics, becoming a follower of Oswald Moseley and the British fascist movement, and because of

The unusual looking Marseal contraption of 1920. The man responsible, Donald Marendaz, led an eventful life. (Vintage Motor Cycle Club)

this was imprisoned in Brixton Jail in 1940. The *Sunday Express* newspaper discovered this and intervened on his behalf due to his heroic efforts during the First World War, and he was subsequently released a few days later. In 1949, he left for South Africa where he started a diesel engine business. He returned to England in 1972 and settled in Asterby, Lincolnshire where he remained until his death in 1988 aged 91.

MAXIM, 1911–1913 (1885–1913)

Maxim Cycle Manufacturing Co., St John's Street & Upper Well Street

In 1885, a 19-year-old Coventry Blacksmith by the name of Arthur James Bonnick established the firm of Bonnick & Co. as cycle manufacturers at King Street. Before long, he and his workforce were selling a range of 'Telephone' safety bicycles, yet because of offering such an extensive range, steadily ran into financial difficulties as the years progressed. William Riley, a Coventry weaver came to his aid in 1890 by purchasing the business, with the agreement that Bonnick would stay on as Manager and retain his name on the products for a term of five years. By 1896, the Riley family sold off their weaving concern, and changed the name of the cycle firm to the Riley Cycle Co. Ltd. At this point, Bonnick was released from his contract at his own request, and soon after had established his second cycle business, called the Maxim Cycle Co. at 11 Court, St John's Street. The following year, he sold this business to the Coventry Wheel Co., but as with the Riley family, was retained as Manager. With the proceeds of the sale he set up yet another cycle firm, called the Plyant Cycle Co., but by November 1898 he was declared bankrupt. After dusting himself down, Bonnick left Coventry behind and moved to Bournemouth where he found work as a cycle agent. From this point onwards, the Maxim Cycle Co. was under the sole control of the Coventry Wheel Co., the latter of which was phased out by 1901. The Maxim concern developed well, producing good quality cycles, but it wasn't for a further ten years that they delved into the motorcycle market. This took the form of a belt-driven three-speed machine powered by a 3½hp TDC engine, but it failed to stand out in the field, lasting only a couple of years.

McKECHNIE, 1921–1922

McKechnie Motors Ltd, Kings Head Chambers, Broadgate

McKechnie Motors Ltd made an appearance for the 1921 season, working out of an address called Kings Head Chambers, in the Broadgate part of the city centre. The Kings Head was a grand Victorian hotel situated on the corner of Hertford Street and Smithford Street, so McKechnie Motors was most probably located at the rear in the old stables. Historically, the Kings Head Hotel, built by George Woodcock, was quite significant in the early development of the British motor industry, as most Coventry meetings staged by the British Motor Syndicate were held there. There is no real indication as to who Mr McKechnie was, but the 1901 census does show a John B. McKechnie of Birmingham aged 28 working in London as an 'Engineer's Tool Maker'. By the early 1920s he may well have returned to the Midlands after gaining experience in the motor industry down south. However, in 1922 the company offered a twin-cylinder leaf-

The McKechnie motorcycle was a short-lived affair. (Vintage Motor Cycle Club)

sprung framed machine powered by a 698cc Coventry Victor flat-twin engine. Although novel in its design, lack of marketing amongst stiff competition failed to convince the public.

McKENZIE, 1921–1928

G.H. McKenzie Autocycles, 26 Warwick Row & St Patrick's Road
The George McKenzie Co., 143 Lower Ford Street & Hill Cross

George H. McKenzie was very active in Coventry in the 1920s working out of addresses all over the city. In 1921 he was seen to be working out of 26 Warwick Row, then later Lower Ford Street, and by 1928, Hill Cross. However, a McKenzie sales brochure of the period provides an address of 'Geo. McKenzie & Co., Sanderstead Works, South Croydon'. The reason for this was because McKenzie was more businessman than mechanical engineer, and his autocycles were actually built for him under license by the Hobart Co. of Coventry, and then sold under the McKenzie name. With frequent trips from London to Coventry it made sense to rent offices in the city as another base. His concept was to provide affordable transport to the masses, offering an ultra-lightweight autocycle fitted with a 170cc Hobart engine. It weighed in at only 75lbs and had a top speed of 28mph. Later models were fitted with 147cc and 175cc Aza motors. Surprisingly, in 1924, McKenzie entered one of his machines in the Ultra-Lightweight TT at the Isle of Man, with rider D.G. Prentice finishing in a very commendable 11th place.
(See also Hobart.)

MEAD, 1911–1916

Coventry Premier Ltd, 10 Read Street, Hillfields, & 8 Lincoln Street

Mead was actually an American-owned cycle company based at Paradise Street, Liverpool, who had been agents of Coventry-built cycles from the turn of the century. In 1911 they approached the Premier Co. of Coventry to produce a motorcycle for them fitted with a 3½hp Precision engine. Following models consisted of 2½hp, 3¾hp and 4¼hp motors, as well the later 6hp and 8hp V-Twin machines. For Mead to have had such an arrangement with Premier would suggest that they were already associated through the bicycle side of the business. Premier themselves had begun manufacturing motorcycles from 1908 so had a reasonable footing in the industry.
(See also Premier.)

Mead had contractual ties with the Premier Co. of Coventry. (Vintage Motor Cycle Club)

MERI, 1911–1913

Meri Cycle & Manufacturing Co., 7 Little Park Street

Nothing is known to date about the motorcycles produced by this company. All that is known is that they are listed in the 1911/12 Kelly's Directory as 'Motorcycle Manufacturers' at 7 Little Park Street. They are also listed at the same address in the 1911/12 and 1912/13 Coventry Spennell Directories. Meri is not listed as a surname in the 1901 census, but may be of foreign origin, seemingly specific to Estonia. Whoever Meri was, his manufacturing company failed to make a stamp in the market, surviving no more than two years.

MIDLAND MOTOR CYLINDER, 1926–1927 (1925–1930)

Midland Motor Cylinder Co., 8 Trafalgar Street

The Midland Motor Cylinder Co. made a very brief entry to the motorcycle market, setting up in premises at Trafalgar Street in the Spon End area of the city in 1925. Unfortunately, nothing is known about the type of machine they developed, but Percy T. Pritchard was seen to have been a key member of the firm. The business is listed under 'Motorcycle Manufacturers' in the 1926/27 Coventry Spennell Directory for one year only, but chances are that they were more of a general engineering concern.

MILLFORD, 1903–1904 & 1933–1937 (1899–1937)

Mills-Fulford Ltd, Progress Works & Crown Works, 287 Stoney Stanton Road

Mills-Fulford first began as 'Cycle Manufacturers' in 1899 at the Crown Cycle Works, Stoney Stanton Road. The men behind the business were James Mills, born in Coventry in 1864, and William Henry Fulford, born in Banbury in 1862. Before long they were specialising in trailers and attachments for bicycles and motorised vehicles, but by 1903 had decided to develop their own motorised machine called the 'Millford'. This consisted of a frame of their own manufacture powered by engines supplied by the Coventry firms Whitley and Hamilton, sharing a stand with the latter at that years Crystal Palace Show. In a contemporary advertisment in *The Motor Cycle*, the company described themselves as 'pioneers of the trailer industry'. Their chosen emblem depicted a milkmaid crossing a ford with a windmill in the background, cleverly taken from the 'Mill' and 'Ford' which formed parts of their surnames. However, after a year the company decided that their real strengths were involved in frames and trailers of which they received much demand for supply. So much so in fact, that as the motor industry accelerated, Mills-Fulford diversified into sidecar

Mills-Fulford were predominately manufacturers of sidecars and trailers, yet did tap into the motorcycle market from time to time during their lifespan. (Coventry Transport Museum)

manufacture, remaining at the top end of their market for years to come. Led by Works Manager Effingham Howe, by 1910 they had patented a damped-spring loaded castor wheel for their sidecars, and then exhibited this at the following years Motor Cycle and Accessories Exhibition at Olympia in London. By 1933, the company was still a huge success, and bought the Rex-Acme concern through Director John T. Chaplin. Under Mills-Fulford, Rex-Acme lightweight motorcycles continued to be sold until 1937 when all business finally ceased.
(See also Rex-Acme.)

MMC, 1897–1904

Motor Manufacturing Co., Motor Mills, Drapers Fields

The Motor Manufacturing Co. was an enterprise founded by Harry J. Lawson in 1897, two years after acquiring the large factory known as the 'Motor Mills'. It was born out of the misrepresentation of Lawson's earlier firm, the Great Horseless Carriage Co., and soon began marketing copies of French Werner motor-bicycles, while building and supplying MMC engines – under license from the French engineers De Dion Bouton. At this time the Works Manager was George Iden. Iden was born at Preston, Lancashire in 1848, and was to become a highly respected Mechanical Engineer when the industry was in its infancy. In 1899 the company received a contract from the War Office to supply a number of 2¼hp MMC tricycles for use in the Boer War, this being the very first occasion where motorcycles were used under actual war conditions. In the spring of 1900, an MMC tricycle ridden by Iden himself took part in the first 1,000-Mile Reliability Trial and faired well. From here onwards the company chose to concentrate more on other projects, while successfully supplying the MMC engine to countless other firms. By 1904 the company was no more, brought on by Lawson's over-ambitious investments, which cost him dear.
(See also Lawson, and Pennington.)

MONOPOLE, 1902–1924 (1890–1937)

Monopole Cycle & Carriage Co., Union Mills, 10–17 Foleshill Road
Monopole Cycle & Motor Co. Ltd, 2 St Mary's Street & 6 Little Park Street

This company was founded in 1890 in the Great Heath area of Coventry as 'Cycle and Carriage Manufacturers'. Who the founders were exactly has unfortunately faded from history, yet it appears that they chose the company name of Monopole because there was a 'Monopole Yard' behind their address of 10–17 Foleshill Road. Monopole first developed a motor-bicycle in 1902 with a 2.5hp Dorman-powered machine, and this was exhibited along with cycles at the Stanley show of that year. It was then a further nine years before they fully delved into motorcycle production, reforming as the Monopole Cycle & Motor Co. They began the new venture by introducing two machines powered by 2½hp and 3½hp Precision engines of a very high

Monopole were another company who were initially in the business of making cycles before turning their hand to motorcycles in 1902. (Vintage Motor Cycle Club)

quality finish. By this time Monopole had moved to an address at St Mary's Street, formerly home to the Palmer Tyre Co. In the early 1920s, like so many others, they fell into difficulty. In an attempt to combat this they added sidecars to their output and by 1936 were back to selling bicycles and carrier cycles at Little Park Street. At this point, their Director was a Mr Herbert J. Skipp. In 1901, Birmingham-born Skipp is listed as living in Coventry and working as a 'Cycle Manufacturer's Clerk', and this may well have been for the Monopole Cycle Co.

MONTGOMERY, 1911–1940 (1892–1955)

Montgomery Motors Ltd, Freeth Street, Gosford Street & Lower Ford Street
Montgomery, W. & Co., Leicester Causeway & Walsgrave Road

The Montgomery motorcycle made its debut in Bury St Edmonds, Suffolk in 1904, a product of an earlier cycle company that was founded in 1892. In 1911, the business relocated to Coventry in a family business arrangement between two brothers, William and James Montgomery. William was born in Manchester in 1881 and can be seen in the 1901 census to be living in Bury St Edmonds as a 'Cycle Manufacturer', specialising in trailers and forecars. Older brother James was born in Manchester in 1869, moving to Coventry during the 1890s, the 1901 census listing him as a 'Cycle & Motor Works Manager'. Ten years later the company of Montgomery Motors Ltd was established at Freeth Street, offering sidecars and machines fitted with 689cc flat-twin engines designed by W.A. Weaver of the Coventry Victor Co. Montgomery also supplied frames to other companies including Packman & Poppe, Coventry Eagle and also to the first Brough-Superiors to be built in 1919. By this time Montgomery had moved to Lower Ford Street and now had a range of machines on offer from 147cc two-strokes to 996cc V-Twin models. In the winter of 1925 their Lower Ford Street Works were devastated by a fire, forcing a move to Leicester Causeway in the Foleshill side of the city. Working from their new premises they picked up where they left off with machines powered by Villiers and JAP engines of various sizes, calling the models 'Greyhound', 'Terrier' and 'Bulldog' amongst others. Production ticked over nicely for the next few years, but a direct hit on their factory from a Luftwaffe bomber in 1940 completely destroyed the factory, and almost the Montgomery name. However, the Birmingham & District Trade Directory of 1954/5 still lists them as 'Motor Cycle Manufacturers', this time located at Walsgrave Road.

(See also Coventry Eagle, Coventry Victor, and P&P.)

The Montgomery Co. began in Bury St Edmunds before making the move to Coventry in 1911. (Coventry Transport Museum)

A Coventry-registered Morton-Adam of 1924. (Mortons Media)

MORTON-ADAM, 1923–1925 (1920–1928)

The Morton-Adam Co., 272 Foleshill Road & 6 Matlock Road, Bishopsgate Green

Starting out as engine makers, Messrs Morton and Adam introduced their first motorcycle in 1923 at their Foleshill Road address. This took the form of a lightweight machine fitted with a 2½hp 246cc two-stroke engine of their own manufacture. It is not known exactly who Mr Adam was, but Mr Morton was thought to be related to the Morton of Morton & Weaver, the men behind the Coventry Victor Motor Co. Later machines offered by Morton-Adam were designed by Harry Sidney and consisted of 248cc and 348cc powered versions, and were among the first overhead camshaft models in England. These continued to be produced until 1925, when the company decided to concentrate on general engineering instead.

(See also Coventry Victor.)

MOUNTAINEER, 1902–1904

Rex Motor Manufacturing Co., Earlsdon Works, Osborne Road

The Mountaineer motor-bicycle was introduced in 1902 by the International Motor Car Co. based at Baker Street in London. Their first machines were fitted with Coventry-built MMC engines before turning production over to the Rex Motor Manufacturing Co. The Mountaineer was really just a heavy-duty cycle with an engine fitted to the main frame. At this time, many manufacturers were offering higher quality machines at a much higher price. Even so, although the Mountaineer offered a machine that was more affordable, it still failed to make the grade. Rex themselves however went on to become main players in the motor industry.

(See also MMC, and Rex.)

Mountaineer motor-bicycles were made by the Rex Co. in Coventry. (Vintage Motor Cycle Club)

MSC, 1906

Motor Safety Co. Ltd, Motor Mills, Drapers Fields

Exactly how many companies Harry J. Lawson founded or floated will probably never be fully known. Yet in 1906, the Motor Safety Co. became yet another business associated with him. In the *Motor Car Journal* of 1906, an article talks of current motorcycle development and in particular the Agricultural Hall Show of that year. The writer states, 'Lawson's Motor Safety Co. exhibited a motor-bicycle with a 1¼hp engine fixed on one side of the rear wheel and a tricycle with motor above the front wheel'. This company had been formed after Lawson had been sentenced for fraud, and although he had served his time, many of his former business associates chose not to further associate themselves with him. Needing financial backing to survive, this lack of support and trust ultimately put an end to the Motor Safety Co. and foiled many of Lawson's future plans in the industry.
(See also Lawson.)

NEW BEESTON

(See Beeston.)

Arthur Lynes built New Era motorcycles for the Era Motor Co. in Liverpool. (Vintage Motor Cycle Club)

NEW ERA, 1920–1922 (1919–1924)

New Era Engineering Co., 38 Moor Street, Earlsdon

As well as producing his own motorcycles, Arthur E. Lynes also assembled machines for other companies. One of these was that of the Era Motor Co., who were based at Miller Street in the Dingle area of Liverpool. Meanwhile, at Moor Street in Earlsdon, Lynes established the New Era Engineering Co., and from 1920 built a 318cc Dalm-powered two-stroke model, followed by a 499cc JAP four-stroke version. By 1922, the arrangement between Lynes and the Era Motor Co. was terminated and Lynes continued with the production of his own machines, as well as a 'Wheatcroft' motorcycle in 1924.
(See also AEL, and Wheatcroft.)

NEWMOUNT, 1929–1933

Newmount Trading Co. Ltd, Reform Chambers, Warwick Row, & Victoria Garage, All Saints Lane, Stoke

The Newmount motorcycle made its debut in 1929, and was offered by the Newmount Trading Co. of Warwick Row, Coventry. Advertised by the company as 'A mount for moderns', these machines were basically German-built Zundapp motorcycles which were then re-badged under the Newmount name, a method often practiced in the industry. It is thought that Newmount was established by J.K. Starley Jnr, after working for many years at the Rover Co. Zundapp, who had been producing motorcycles since 1917 at Nuremberg, only had dealings

The Newmount Trading Co. was believed to have been founded by J.K. Starley Jnr. (Vintage Motor Cycle Club)

A Newmount model of 1929 – basically a revamped Zundapp machine. (Mortons Media)

with Newmount in Britain, with the exception of Coventry-based Rudge who supplied the German firm with engines. Interestingly, in 1931, the Newmount Trading Co. entered a 350cc Newmount machine at the Isle of Man TT, powered by a Python engine, which was made by the Rudge Co. Ridden by Irishman C.H. Manders it failed to complete the course. Newmount also offered a 200cc model, which they sold for £36 until 1933.

(See also Rudge.)

NEW STAR, 1919–1921

New Star Co., Broad Lane, Tile Hill

As well as marketing their motorcycles under the Coventry Star and Star marques, the New Star Co. of Broad Lane also sold their machines under their actual company name. These were simple belt-driven machines of two-speeds, powered by a 269cc Villiers engine. The New Star models were nothing out of the ordinary, which is why the company ultimately lasted less than two years.

(See also Coventry Star, and Star.)

NOBLE-PRECISION, 1911–1912 (1911–1925)

Noble, Alfred & Co., Stoneleigh Works, 5 Hill Street

Alfred Noble set himself up in business in 1911 as 'Cycle & Motorcycle Manufacturers' at an address known as Stoneleigh Works at Hill Street. It is also thought that he developed a car at around the same period of which very little is known. His motorcycle was a belt-driven machine using Druid forks and powered by a 3½hp Precision engine. Two entries in the 1901 census may shed light on who Noble was: Alfred Noble aged 18 of Coventry was working in the city as a 'Clerk for a Railway', and Alfred Noble aged 20 of Nottinghamshire was working in Gainsborough as an 'Engine Erector Apprentice'. Whoever he was, Noble's overall operation was small and production on a limited scale, and soon after, he concentrated on general mechanical engineering and repair.

A Noble-Precision motorcycle of 1912, the final year of their production. (Mortons Media)

NORTON, 1904–1905

Norton Cycle & Motor Co., 3 Binley Road

Not to be confused with the James Norton motorcycle of Birmingham, the Norton Cycle & Motor Co. made a brief entry in the 1904 and 1905 Coventry Directories as 'Cycle & Motorcycle Manufacturers' at Binley Road. The man responsible was Stephen Herbert Norton (b. 1864) who had previously worked as a Secretary for another Coventry cycle firm for many years, but sadly nothing is known to date about the machines he built. His younger brother, John Norton, may also have been involved with the company, as the 1901 census shows that he too had a background in the industry, listed as a 'Clerk in a Cycle Company'. There are also a number of other Norton's in Coventry at this time involved in the cycle trade, so it would seem likely that the origins of this particular company go back further. After 1905 however, the trail runs dry.

OMEGA, 1919–1927 (1918–1927)

W.J. Green Ltd, Omega Works, Croft Road, Hill Street, Swan Lane & Little Park Street

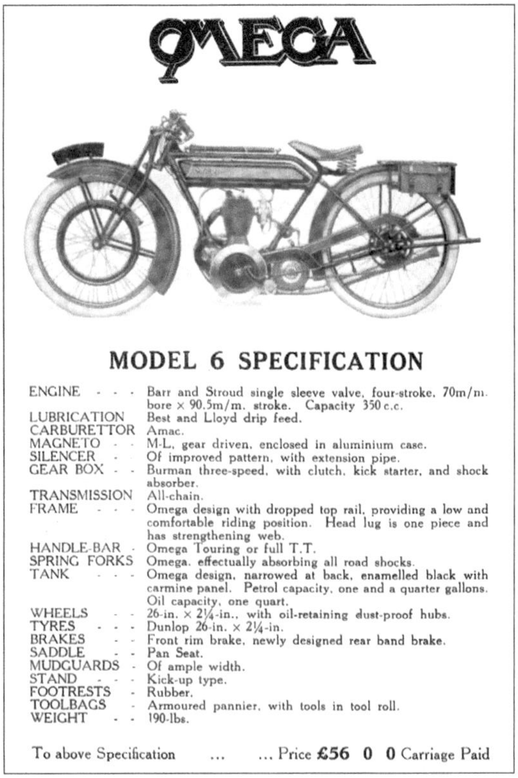

William Green worked for both Humber and Premier before starting up his own company in 1918. (Coventry Transport Museum)

William James Green was born in Nottingham in April 1876. On leaving school he joined the Humber Co. at Beeston, before transferring to Coventry in 1896. By 1905, he was contracted to the Premier Co. as 'Overseas Sales Manager' travelling to many exotic destinations to drum up sales. It was also while at Premier that Green married his Secretary, Margaret Hailstone in July 1906. Margaret was the daughter of J.E. Hailstone who later formed half of Ravenhall & Hailstone, the Coventry motorcycle makers (1922–25). At this time the Green family were residing at a large house on Binley Road. After the war in 1918, Green decided to start a business of his own making motorcycles. He chose the name of 'Omega' for his machines, found premises initially at Croft Road, and registered the company as 'W.J. Green Ltd – Motor Engineers'. Early on, Green developed an engine of his own making, and a motorcycle, and exhibited such products at the 1919 International Cycle, Motor Cycle and Accessories Exhibition at Olympia in London. Apart from making his own motorcycles, Green also built sidecars from 1920 and a three-wheeled car between 1925 and 1927. He also extended his business opportunities by supplying machines to Gamage of London, and York of Germany.

(See also Gamage, Humber, Omegette, Premier, R&H, and York.)

OMEGETTE, 1921

W.J. Green Ltd, Omega Works, Swan Lane

William Green sold the majority of his motorcycles under the Omega name, but in 1921, he also introduced a machine which he oddly labelled the 'Omegette'. This was a chain-driven lightweight Burman two-speed model fitted with a 269cc Villiers engine. Not too many were made and Green soon moved on to other projects.

(See also Omega.)

OSBORN, 1901

F.J. Osborn, Coventry

A surprise entry to this list, but the 1931 book *Early Days in the British Motor Cycle Industry* states:

Frederick Osborn went on to make O.E.C. motorcycles at Gosport – a business which lasted until 1954. (Coventry Transport Museum)

> This was a period when experts often put together special machines with large engines, chiefly for track racing. Mr F.J. Osborn, the designer of the O.E.C. motor-bicycle, built a typical one at Coventry in 1901, with a 4-hp engine fitted in the 'Minerva' position. Mr Osborn had, at that time, some useful experience in motor cycle building for he had erected a number of motor bath-chairs, adopting one of Lawson's schemes with the engine at one side of the front wheel which it drove through an epicyclical gear. These machines were built at Coventry but did not find a market.

This is supported in T.E. Crowley's 1973 book *Discovering Old Motorcycles*, in which he states, 'by 1901, other firms of note to launch into motorcycle production around the same time included New Imperial and O.E.C., a racing 4.hp design by F.J. Osborn, built in Coventry'. Osborn's full name was Frederick John Osborn, and after his time in Coventry he later found works at Gosport (1901–1954) producing the O.E.C. make, which stood for Osborn Engineering Co. The 1901 census does in fact reveal a John Osborn of Coventry aged 36, living and working in the city as an 'Engineers Fitter', but whether this is the same man or a relative is unclear.

PAYNE & BATES

(See Godiva.)

PENNINGTON, 1895–1899 (1894–1902)

E.J. Pennington, Humber Works, Lower Ford Street, & Motor Mills, Drapers Fields

Edward Joel Pennington was born in Indiana, America in 1858. In the 1890s he became actively involved in the early days of the American motor industry, inventing fanciful designs that were, more often than not, way beyond their supposed capabilities. These were known to have included two primitive motor-bicycles (a tandem and a single), a tricycle, and a quadricycle called the 'Victoria'. In 1895, Harry J. Lawson became aware of Pennington's work, and invited him over to England to become part of his newly formed British Motor Syndicate. By now, Lawson had acquired factories and a workforce in Coventry, and it was his intention to take Pennington's ambitious designs and make them a reality, while making himself extremely rich in the process. So in October 1895, Lawson met Pennington in the Metropole Hotel in London, and paid the American a massive £100,000 for the British rights to his portfolio of designs, including motorised bicycles, tricycles, motorcars, a fire-engine, and even a military gun-car. Work began straight away at the Humber Works at Lower Ford Street under the supervision of T.W. Blumfield, with testing taking place at the Butts cycle track. In June 1896, it was announced that the first British-built motor-bicycle, a Pennington-Humber, had been produced in Coventry. However, all of a sudden things took a drastic turn for the worse when fire engulfed the Humber factory, destroying vehicles ready for sale and all the supporting blueprints. Undeterred, Lawson quickly moved production to the 'Motor Mills', and had Pennington, Blumfield and other principal members of the workforce recreate his designs from memory. Pennington wasted no time that year, registering no less than twenty-eight patent applications. Most of these were outrageous in their claims, but Pennington was also quite a showman, and had the knack of charming people of wealth to subscribe to his ideas and advertised extensively in the British press. One such claim was that his motorcycle could leap over rivers, and he had promotional pictures created to demonstrate this. The 1951 book *Motor Cycle Cavalcade* by Ixion states: 'The Pennington was one of the less grotesque imaginations of that notorious invader, who used plain steel tubing devoid of radiating fins for his cylinder barrels and claimed that a patent "long mingling spark" endowed all his products with fantastic power.' The reality of Pennington's designs, however, were usually machines that did not work well at all, let alone propel their riders through the air. By 1900, Lawson lost patience, and attempted to sue Pennington. The American was one step ahead though and fled back to his homeland with all his wealth intact. He continued his antics in America with designs for aviation, while Lawson was imprisoned on charges of fraud after failing to repay his key investors. Apparently, Pennington died suddenly in March 1911 at the age of 53 at Springfield, Massachusetts, a broken man, so somewhere down the line it would appear that his past caught up with him. Yet in 1907, Ernest Courtis, who worked under Pennington at Coventry from 1895, wrote, 'Mr E.J. Pennington was a good man to his workpeople, and highly respected by all of them, and undoubtedly was a first-class mechanic.' History generally recalls Edward Joel Pennington as a fraudster and conman, yet there is still no mistake that however exaggerated his inventions were, he was still very influential in the early years of the British motor industry.

(See also Humber, Lawson, and Pennington-Sturmey.)

Workers on a floor of the 'Motor Mills' in Coventry busy with the production of Pennington designs. (Coventry Transport Museum)

The Flying Pennington Cycle.

By the use of an inclined plane, rising to the height of about two feet only, the **Pennington Bicycle** has been made to jump the extraordinary distance of 65 feet. With a flying start it was "charged" up the incline at very high speed, alighting on the rear wheel first, and the writer was able to keep his seat without difficulty. As a test of the motive power, strength, and stability of the machine, and the resiliency of the tyres, I think this feat must be regarded as conclusive.

Pennington claimed that his motor-bicycle could literally leap rivers. (Coventry Transport Museum)

An 1895 Pennington motor-bicycle being tested by Mr Fergusson at the Butts Cycle Track. (Coventry Transport Museum)

Fergusson (front) and colleague demonstrate a Pennington motor tandem. (Coventry Transport Museum)

PENNINGTON-STURMEY, 1896

E.J. Pennington & H. Sturmey, Motor Mills, Drapers Fields

Page 17 in *A History of the World's Motorcycles* (1966) by Richard Hough and L.J.K. Setright shows a drawing of this motor-bicycle driven by an engine positioned above the front wheel. The caption reads: 'A more rational extension of the Pennington principle, as designed by Sturmey of the Autocar'. Henry Sturmey was one of the founder members of the British Motor Syndicate, and was involved in the very first John O'Groats to Lands End run in a British-built Daimler in October 1897. Considering that Pennington was largely based at the 'Motor Mills' from 1896, it would be safe to assume that this experimental machine was built there by the Humber workforce under Lawson's supervision, yet it's doubtful it ever reached the production stage.

(See also Humber, Lawson, and Pennington.)

PERKS & BIRCH, 1899–1901

Perks & Birch Ltd, Rockland Works, Eagle Street, Foleshill

Edwin Perks and Frank Birch* shook the motoring world in 1899 with a revolutionary design that was later taken up by the Singer Motor Co. It was called the 'Motor Wheel', being an aluminum-alloy wheel containing a single-cylinder engine unit and fuel tank, and designed to simply replace the front or rear wheel of a pedal-cycle. Built at small works behind a house known as 'The Rocklands' on Foleshill Road, the motor-wheel was tested on a cycle and tricycle on the surrounding streets. The manufacturing rights were then bought by Singer, who also acquired the services of its inventors, Perks as a Motor Engineer, and Birch as Foreman in the Motor Department. In his 1951 book *Motor Cycles History & Development*, C.F. Caunter writes, 'an unorthodox but successful design of this period, and one that formed a precedent for a design half a century later, was the Singer Motor-Wheel, originally patented by Perks & Birch of Coventry in 1899'. Perks was born in Kingswinford, Staffordshire in 1867. Sometime in the 1880s he moved to Coventry and like so many others found work in the thriving cycle industry. During the 1890s while working for the Beeston Motor Co., he became more involved with the development of motorised transport, which ultimately brought him and Birch together. The 1901 census shows

Edwin Perks pictured on a Perks & Birch 'motor-wheeled' tricycle, soon to be adopted by the Singer Co. (Coventry Transport Museum)

him aged 34, working in Coventry as a 'Motor Engineer' and residing at 5 Stoney Stanton Road. Frank Birch was born at Spencer Avenue, Coventry on 24 November 1871. He too gained employment at one of the city's many cycle manufacturers before teaming up with Perks. The 1901 census shows him aged 30, working as an 'Automobile Engineer' and living at 77 Widdrington Road. It's not known exactly how many years that Perks and Birch worked for Singer, but by 1920, Frank Birch opened up a cycle shop at Spon Street, and by 1933 had established a motor garage at Conduit Yard, the site where the first Coventry Motette was built in 1897. At the same time, Perks looks to have retired, residing at Glen Lea, 26 Binley Road. He died at the age of 89 in 1956 and is buried at London Road cemetery along with his wife, Susan Jane Louise Perks.

*Frank Birch was not connected to the George Eliot motor-bicycle built from 1902–1905 as often thought. This was built in Nuneaton by John North Birch (1865–1945) of Foleshill, who emigrated to New Zealand in 1905 and later founded the Carlton and Marlborough car companies.

(See also Singer.)

PHELON-HUMBER, 1901–1905

Humber Ltd, Humber Works, Lower Ford Street

When Humber Ltd first began experimenting with motorised transport under the ownership of Harry Lawson, by default, they associated themselves with many other companies and individuals, testing out designs and ideas. J.C. Phelon first worked with his nephew Harry Rayner from 1896, building quadricycles at Cleckheaton in Yorkshire. They later developed a motorcycle fitted with a De Dion type sloping engine mounted in the front down tube, and a unique all-chain drive system. This concept was offered to a number of investors, but only Lawson took an interest. Back in Coventry, Lawson directed the Humber workforce to build their own 2hp machine based on the Phelon & Rayner design, and this by most accounts gradually formed the basis of future Humber motorcycle development.

(See also Humber, and Lawson.)

POWERFUL, 1903–1906

H.W. Clarke & Co., Gosford Street

The 'Powerful' motorcycle was first released to the public in 1903 by Harold Wibmer Clark of Brighton (b. 1878) at an address in Gosford Street. At a time when most companies were powering their machines with De Dion or Minerva motors, Clark opted to use a 2¼ hp Buchet engine, inclined and mounted above the downtube inside the frame. Buchet were another French company specialising in the supply of engines, but were also active in the development of powered airships from 1896. Clark was known to have been in Coventry from at least 1899, taking out three motor related patents whilst living at 'Daisy Bank' on Middleborough Road. His activities after 1906 are so far unknown.

H.W. Clarke offered the 'Powerful' motor-bicycle for just three years only. (Vintage Motor Cycle Club)

POWER-PAK, 1950–1956

The Power-Pak Engineering Co., Coventry

An advertisment from the *Motor Cycling Magazine* of 27 October 1955 reads: 'A Mo-Ped from Coventry, a British-built light autocycle announced by Power-Pak Engineering Co. Ltd for the coming season'. The article goes on to say that the company were planning to build 1,000 machines a week thanks to the acquisition of a large and modern factory in Coventry, but where this was exactly is unclear. The Power-Pak was basically a pedal-assisted 49cc 'clip-on' two-stroke motor which would be attached over the rear wheel of a standard bicycle. They were priced at £54 for a standard model and £64 for the de-luxe version, and could reach a top speed of 30mph at an impressive 200mpg. It is believed that the Power-Pak Engineering Co. were a subsidiary of Sinclair-Goddard & Co.

P&P, 1922–1930

Packman & Poppe Ltd, 64 Moor Street & 37 Ford Street, Earlsdon

Packman & Poppe Ltd started out in 1922 at premises in Moor Street, Earlsdon. It was founded by Gilmour Packman and Erling Poppe, the son of Peter Poppe of White & Poppe fame. Packman was born in Rochester, Kent in 1899, and Poppe born at Steyr in Austria, also in 1899, while his father worked there designing rifles. Erling studied engineering at Birmingham University before joining Packman, and together they designed and marketed the P&P 'Silent Three' motorcycle, built by the Montgomery Co. under contract. This machine was fitted with

A P&P motorcycle of 1923. The man seated is most probably either Packman or Poppe. (Mortons Media)

a 350cc Barr & Stroud sleeve-valve engine, with Packman & Poppe claiming it to be the 'quietest motorcycle in the world'. Production went well until disaster and controversy hit the company in 1925. The story has it that on one day in June, Gilmour Packman got into a fight with a 'works colleague' whose identity remains unclear. The fight was so intense that both crashed into shelving which was holding a quantity of heavy silencers. The impact forced one of the silencers to come smashing down on Packman's head, killing him instantly. After a lengthy inquest, the law courts put the incident down as a freak industrial accident, much to the dismay of the Packman family. This tragedy was followed some years later by a fire at the Montgomery Works in Coventry, where the P&P motorcycle was being built under license using Montgomery frames. This brought about the end of the P&P machine, and Poppe went on to work for Rover, Dennis and then BSA, becoming their Chief Designer by 1946. He later went on to work for Douglas as Technical Director until his retirement.
(See also Montgomery, Rover, White, and Poppe.)

PREMIER, 1908–1920 (1875–1923)

Premier Cycle Co., 10 Read Street, Hillfields
Coventry Premier Co., 10 Read Street, Hillfields, & 8 Lincoln Street

The first Premier motorcycle was built in 1908 at their large Read Street factory, but the company's roots took hold over thirty years earlier. In 1875, two men named Hillman and Herbert founded a cycle company at South Street. William Hillman was born at Lewisham, Kent in 1847 and worked alongside the likes of James Starley, Josiah Turner and George Singer at the very beginnings of Coventry's involvement with cycle development. William Herbert (the brother of Alfred Herbert of Machine Tool fame) was born in Royal Leamington Spa in 1858 and took care of the financial side of the company. Yorkshire-born George B. Cooper, a cycle racer, then joined the firm in 1896 to form Hillman, Herbert & Cooper. With such a good grounding in the cycle industry, it wasn't until 1908 that the Premier Cycle Co. (as they were now called) entered the motorcycle market. Their first model was built using a 3½hp White & Poppe engine of belt-drive. Before long Premier were producing their own complete machines, building their own engines, frames and forks in-house. The company's 1913 sales brochure offered a range of five motorcycles of different engine sizes, single engines and accessories. The brochure also named the company Directors, who at that time were Alexander J. Rotherham and Kenneth Rotherham of watch-making fame, W.H. Hughes, and W.J. Green, later the founder of Omega motorcycles. At this time, Premier had also added motorcars and sidecars to their output of cycles and motorcycles. The business continued through the First World

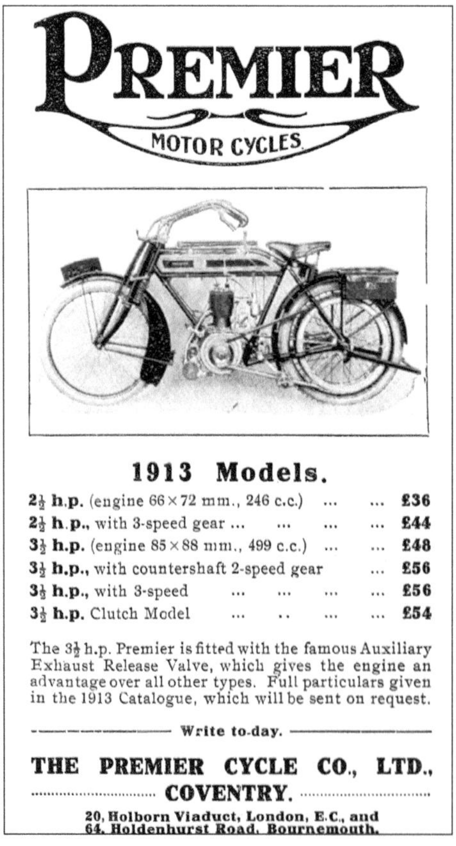

The Premier Co. offered a range of motorcycles for the 1913 season. (Coventry Transport Museum)

An advertisment for Enoch West's Progress motor-bicycle of 1902. (Vintage Motor Cycle Club

War on a reduced scale, but afterwards they struggled to get back on track. A change of name to the Coventry Premier Co. wasn't enough to inspire potential buyers, and soon after the entire business was bought by the neighbouring Singer Motor Co.
(See also Coventry Premier, Mead, and Sparkbrook.)

PROGRESS, 1897–1908 (1888–1914)

Progress Cycle & Motor Co., 412–420 Stoney Stanton Road, Foleshill
E.J. West & Co. Ltd, Foleshill Road

Enoch John West was born at Exhall on the outskirts of Coventry in 1864. After a brief stint as a house painter, he became an apprentice at the Singer Cycle Co. before becoming part of the cycle makers Calcott Bros & West in 1888. At the age of 27, in 1891 he began manufacturing cycles of his own under the name of E.J. West & Co. at Foleshill Road, in partnership with a Mr William Harris. This soon became the Progress Cycle Co. and by 1897 they began designing and building motorised transport. Their first motorcycles consisted of Minerva, MMC or Antoine engines attached to the down-tube of one of their own heavy-duty cycles. By 1902, the company had produced some 150 Voiturettes, motorcycles, quadricycles and tricycles, and from 1899 to 1903, had produced some 500 cars. This was only an output of two or three a week, yet for quite a small concern it resulted in an impressive and steady amount of sales. In July 1905, West Ltd was formed, and two years later reformed again as West-Aster. This went into liquidation in 1908, and with it saw the end of any further motorcycle production. Residing by now at Clifton House on the Foleshill Road, West remained active, building Heron-Aster, Academy and Pilot cars, and by 1912 he was manufacturing cycle cars under the West and Ranger trade names. After the war he became a Works Manager at the Coventry engine makers, White & Poppe. He died at Kenilworth in Warwickshire in 1937.
(See also Ranger, Singer, and White & Poppe.)

QUADRANT, 1907–1911 (1883–1934)

Quadrant Motor Co. Ltd, Moor Street, Earlsdon

The Quadrant name was first used in 1883 at Sheepcote Street in Birmingham with the manufacture of tricycles. The company was founded by brothers Walter John Lloyd and William Lloyd, and gained a worthy reputation for the quality of the cycles they produced. In the early 1900s they were joined by William Priest and Tom Silver, who helped the company evolve into the manufacture of motorcycles, initially using Minerva engines. By 1907 the company fell into financial difficulties and the receivers were called in. A new enterprise was formed by Priest and Silver as the Quadrant Motor Co. Ltd, and production was transferred to Moor Street in

The Quadrant Co. Ltd relocated from Birmingham to Coventry in 1907. (Vintage Motor Cycle Club)

the Earlsdon area of Coventry. In 1910 William Pollard represented Quadrant as rider at the Isle of Man TT but was forced to retire early. In Earlsdon they continued to manufacture cycles and motorcycles until 1911 when they opted to return to Birmingham at Lawley Street. However, cycle production remained in Coventry at Foleshill Road under the management of Edward O'Brien until the 1930s.

RAGLAN, 1902–1903 (1894–1906)

Raglan Cycle Co., Raglan Works, Raglan Street

The Raglan Cycle Co. was set up in the 1890s by Messrs Taylor, Cooper and Bednall. These three enterprising men had first built an electric car at the imposing Raglan Works in 1894 from a design by Garrard & Blumfield. By 1899, it is reported that they built a modified version of the International Benz motorcar with an announcement that twelve would be made initially, yet nothing really materialised. In 1902, Raglan developed a basic motor-bicycle fitted with a 2hp Clement-Garrard engine, and a forecar powered by a 3¾hp motor – both being exhibited at the Stanley Show. A Birmingham company by the same name developed motorcycles from 1909–1913 but whether they had any connections to the Coventry cycle concern is not known.

R&H, 1922–1925

Hailstone & Ravenhall, 132 Clay Lane, Stoke

The R&H motorcycle was introduced in 1922 by George William Ravenhall and John Edward Hailstone. Ravenhall was born in 1877 at Birmingham. He worked as a 'Press Tool Maker' there during his early career, before making the short trip to Coventry in 1910. He soon found employment as a Works Manager at the Rover Cycle Co., where motorcycles had been marketed since 1903. In 1912 he led a team of engineers to Russia, training the locals in the skills of motorcycle production methods until 1915. Back in Britain with Rover he captained the works team in competitions at Brooklands and the Isle of Man TT, and in 1921, won a gold medal at the International Six Days Trial. In 1922 he formed an alliance with a

Right: George Ravenhall during his Rover days teaching Russian workers motorcycle production methods. (Ron Ravenhall)

Below: George Ravenhall (middle rear) with the Rover Works racing team. (Ron Ravenhall)

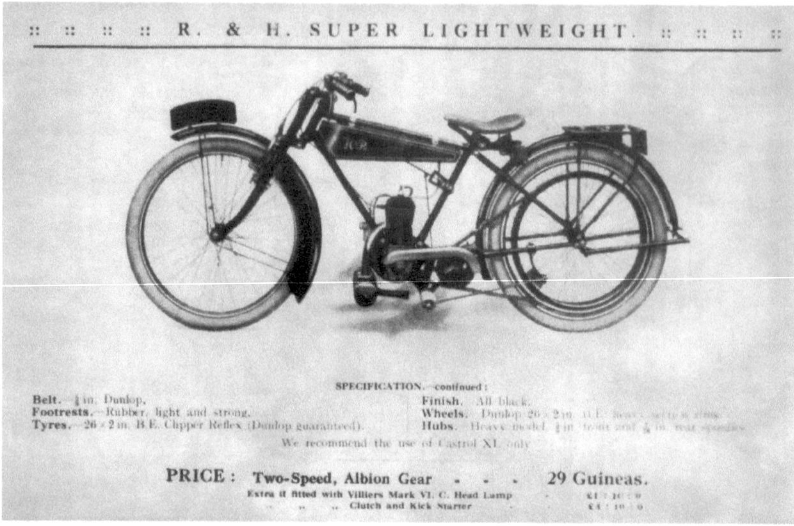

The R&H Super Lightweight motorcycle of 1922. (Coventry Transport Museum)

Kenilworth Draper called Hailstone. Hailstone provided funds and premises at Clay Lane and left the rest to Ravenhall, who was completely responsible for the design and production of the motorcycle. This took the form of a 'Super Lightweight' machine fitted with a 147cc Villiers engine. Being such a small concern, it is believed that only around thirty machines were ever built and sold between 1922 and 1925. Ravenhall's links with the motorcycle industry were not entirely finished though, as he returned to tool-making for the Coventry Eagle Company. And of Hailstone? The 1933/34 *Coventry Directory* listed him as J. E. Hailstone Ltd., 'Drapers and Milliners' at 132a Clay Lane and 177 Walsgrave Road. His daughter also married W. J. Green, the creator of the Omega machine.
(See also H&R, and Rover.)

RED ARNO, 1914–1915 (1906–1915)
Arno Motor Co., Gosford Street

For 1914, the Arno Motor Co. offered motorcycles under the 'Red Arno' name, as well as standard Arno machines. These were 3½hp, 493cc and 4½hp, 585cc machines that derived from their TT model. The 'Red' referred to the colour of these competition racers that saw reasonable success on the Isle of Man. The production of this marque ended in 1915, along with the rest of the business.
(See also Arno.)

REGENT, 1919–1920
Coventry Victor Motor Co. Ltd, 137–139 Cox Street
Regent Motors Ltd, 116 Victoria Street, London

Regent Motors was set up in London in 1919 by a group of ex-First World War servicemen. They approached Morton & Weaver of the Coventry Victor Motor Co., who assembled for them a 689cc flat-twin sleeve-valve machine of their own making. This was then shipped down to Regent where they completed the units with other outsourced parts, and when finished, added the Regent transfer. Apparently it was the intention of the company to produce some

3,000 complete machines a year, but for whatever reason they over-speculated, and the firm dissolved soon after. Coventry Victor prospered however, and even adopted the Regent name, selling Coventry Regent machines for a limited period, no doubt the cast-offs that were by now surplus to requirements following Regent's closure.
(See also Coventry Regent, and Coventry Victor.)

REMINGTON, 1919–1920 (1909–1934)

Remington Cycle Co. Ltd, and the Remington Motor Co. Ltd, 201 Foleshill Road

This company began life as cycle manufacturers at an address known as 'Trinity Churchyard' in 1909. This location could only refer to the area around Holy Trinity Church in the very centre of Coventry, yet where the actual factory was is open for debate. Sometime later, Remington moved to units at 201 Foleshill Road, an area heavily populated by similar businesses. By 1919 the company had become more of a general engineering concern, and began to build cars and motorcycles on a limited scale. Production of cycles was steadily phased out and the company concentrated on cars and engineering until closure in 1934. It is not altogether clear who Mr Remington was, but the 1901 census reveals two strong possibilities – a Mr Alfred A. Remington aged 23, born in Sutton Coldfield, working in Erdington as a 'Motor Car Draughtsman', and Mr Alfred C. Remington aged 27, working as a 'Cycle Maker' in Leicester.

REVERE, 1915–1922

W.H. Whitehouse & Co., 16 Friars Road

The Revere motorcycle was said to have been assembled for Walter Whitehouse by the Sparkbrook Co. of Coventry from 1915. Considering the First World War was in full swing, it seems surprising that he would chose to start a business during such hard times, yet somehow it lasted. These machines were powered by 2½hp 269cc single-cylinder two-stroke engines, with options of direct-drive, and two- or three-speed gears and sold from £35. The origins of Whitehouse are not clear but he may have been involved in cycle manufacture prior to 1915 in Coventry. He also marketed motorcycles under his own name from 1919 to 1920, but all production ceased in 1922, and nothing is known of his whereabouts from then on.
(See also Sparkbrook, and Whitehouse.)

REX, 1901–1922 (1898–1933)

Rex Motor Manufacturing Co., Earlsdon Works, Osborne Road

There have been many world-famous motoring companies founded in Coventry, yet some have been seriously overlooked in terms of innovation and manufacturing achievements. The Rex Co. is perhaps the best example of this, being one of the first motoring firms to be established in the city at the beginning of the twentieth century. The Rex story begins in 1901, when the Birmingham Motor Manufacturing & Supply Co. merged with one of their suppliers; Coventry-based Allard, establishing a new enterprise called the Rex Motor Manufacturing Co. at works in Osborne Road. The name Rex derived from the Latin word for 'King', and was chosen by its founders, brothers George, William, Arthur and Alfred Pilkington, four Birmingham engineers who had previously managed a tube metal business. Advertising themselves as 'the king of British motors', in 1902 Rex enlarged their works and set about building a variety of three- and four-wheeled cars while also introducing their first motorcycle, a 247cc four-stroke machine. The company soon added ex-work colleagues Harold and Billy Williamson to the ranks, combining their skills to design and build quality machines of various

Detail of an early Rex engine. (Coventry Transport Museum)

capacities. The firm also cleverly devised a way that people could part-exchange their older machines, riding a new motorcycle away for half the price. By 1906 their reputation intensified, and in their new season sales brochure they stated, 'The Rex is entirely British made. The Rex Co. has the largest output of any motor cycle firm in the world. It is a point of historical interest that one of the very first automobile engines ever built in England was made in this factory nine years ago'. In 1907, Rex built a motorcycle for Muriel Hind, the pioneering female motorcyclist. Hind had become something of a celebrity, winning many trophies in motorcycle trials, but she was also as a journalist, testing machines for companies and then writing up reviews. The Rex Co. were very confident in their products and saw Hind as an ideal way to conquer the growing female motor market if they offered her the right machine. The result was the 'Blue Devil', a 5hp V-Twin, which she became very fond of, later writing up a glowing report. Hind also became fond of Richard (Dick) Lord of the Rex Co., and in 1912 they were married and moved to Wall Hill on the outskirts of Coventry. By this time, much had changed at Rex, as a year earlier there had been a boardroom disagreement, resulting in the Williamson brothers leaving the company. Billy Williamson had been Managing Director at Rex, yet the dispute with the Pilkington family was too great, forcing him to leave. Within a matter of weeks he had established his very own motorcycle business, the Williamson Motor Co., a stone's throw from his former employers at Moor Street. Harold Williamson supported his brother, but found alternative employment as Sales Manager at the Singer Works. At the outbreak of war in 1914, William Pilkington also left the company by selling his interests to a Mr George Hemmingway. Hemmingway introduced sidecars to the firm's output while continuing to sell the motorcycles under the Rex name until 1922. In this year the company merged with the Coventry Acme Motor Co. to become the Rex-Acme Motor Manufacturing Co., based at the original Rex factory at Osborne Road.

(See also Acme, Allard, and Rex-Acme.)

The Rex engine testing shop. (Coventry Transport Museum)

A rare image capturing employees in the Rex finishing shop. (Coventry Transport Museum)

Further detail of the Rex power unit. (Coventry Transport Museum)

Rex workers pictured at the rear of the Earlsdon Works. (Coventry Transport Museum)

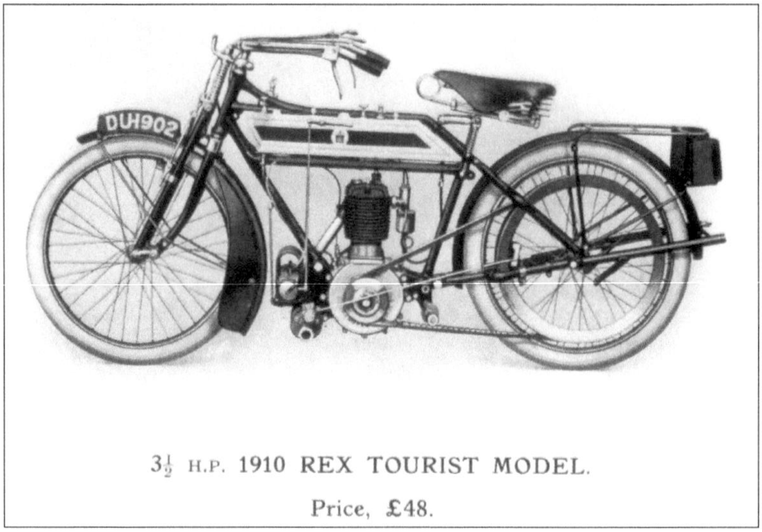

The Rex Tourist Trophy model of 1910. (Coventry Transport Museum)

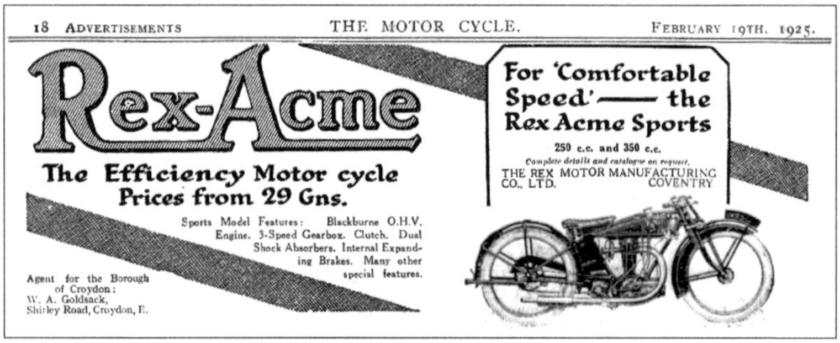

Rex merged with the Acme Co. in 1922. (Coventry Transport Museum)

REX-ACME, 1922–1933

Rex-Acme Motor Manufacturing Co. Ltd, Osborne Road, Earlsdon
Mills-Fulford (1932) Ltd, 283 Stoney Stanton Road

In 1922, the Rex Motor Co. bought their way into the Coventry Acme Motor Co., establishing the Rex-Acme Motor Co. at Osborne Road, Earlsdon. Both Rex and Acme had earned years of experience in the motoring field as both had been founded at the turn of the century, and were at the forefront of pioneering development. With such a background and combination of engineering excellence, it wasn't long before the first Rex-Acme was released. This took the form of a lightweight machine powered by a 247cc two-stroke Morris engine, and was soon followed by a range of machines fitted with JAP, CAM, and Blackburne motors of various sizes. By 1925, the company had become more active on the racing circuit and were joined by Walter Handley, their most successful rider. Handley, who went on to become Works Manager and then later Director, won both Junior and Ultra-Lightweight classes at the 1925 Isle of Man TT, the company's first 'double' victory. The following year saw Handley and his works team develop their racing machines with a 348cc ohv Blackburne model, and it was on this bike that he gained the world's one-hour record by covering 91.21 miles in sixty minutes. More victories followed during 1927 and 1928 but Handley parted with the company and moved on to new pastures. The company continued to offer a wide range of models fitted with Villiers, Blackburne and JAP engines, and even revived the 'Speed King' sports model from their pre-war Rex days. Like so many other companies, the beginning of the 1930s saw tough times

for Rex-Acme, and in 1932 they were bought by Mills-Fulford Ltd, the Coventry sidecar makers. Under their new owners the remaining workforce developed some machines fitted with 346cc-500cc JAP and 249cc Villiers engines, but it was not enough to lift the business and they were closed indefinitely the following year.
(See also Acme, Mills-Fulford, and Rex.)

REX-JAP, 1911–1914

Rex Motor Manufacturing Co., Earlsdon Works, Osborne Road

These machines were built by the Rex Motor Manufacturing Co. from 1911 under a contract agreed by the Premier Motor Co. of Birmingham. They were then marketed by Premier and consisted of a range of V-Twins and singles powered by 6hp and 8hp JAP engines. The outbreak of war, however, saw an early end to this arrangement. Although often assumed, this Premier operation had no connections with the Premier Motor Co. in Coventry except, ironically, for the fact that at one point both were involved in a court battle concerning naming rights in 1909.
(See also Rex.)

RILEY, 1899–1906 (1890–1969)

Riley Cycle Co. Ltd, St Nicholas Street
Riley Motor Co. Ltd, Castle Works, Cook Street; City Works, St Nicholas Street; Cunard Works, Aldbourne Road; & Durbar Avenue, Foleshill

Although Riley was another famous motoring name to come out of Coventry, their involvement with motorcycle production only lasted some seven years. The Riley Cycle Co. was established in 1890 at St Nicholas Street by William Riley. The son of a Coventry weaver, Riley was born in 1851 and on leaving school became an apprentice at his father's mill where he remained for a good number of years. During the 1880s he became friends with the cycling journalist Henry Sturmey (1857–1930), which furthered his interest in the local development of cycles. In 1890, Riley bought the assets of the Bonnick Cycle Co. (est. 1885), retaining the services of Arthur Bonnick as Works Manager and E.J. Bakewell as Sales Manager at King Street. When Bonnick left in 1896, the company became the Riley Cycle Co. with brothers Herbert and Basil Riley joining the family business, Herbert placed as General Manager. William was also joined by his sons Victor, Allan and Percy, with Stanley and Cecil Riley coming in later. In 1898, Percy and Stanley Riley took the lead in

The Riley family had their origins embedded in the Coventry Weaving Industry until 1890, when William Riley bought a cycle company. (Coventry Transport Museum)

Forecars built by companies such as Riley enabled families to escape to the countryside. (Coventry Transport Museum)

developing motorised transport for the company in the form of a De Dion Bouton type car. The following year they exhibited a 'Royal Riley' quadricycle and tricycle fitted with 2¼hp Minerva and Cudell engines at the National Cycle Show, and by 1900, a 3½hp MMC-powered machine. The Riley Engine Co. was established in 1903 by Percy and Victor, and from this point onwards all vehicles were fitted with engines of their own making, including their new 'Moto-Bi' 2hp, 2¾hp and 3½hp motorcycles priced from £45. By 1906 Riley offered a 6hp 800cc V-Twin machine, but this would be their last production motorcycle until the 1930s, opting to concentrate on car development instead. The founder of this hugely successful company, William Riley, died on 17 January 1944 at Kenilworth at the age of 93. Such was his dedication to the Riley concern that it wasn't until he was 86 that he finally retired from the board.

(See also Ayton-Riley.)

ROULETTE, 1911–1914 (1890–1919)

Roulette Cycle Co., 84 Gosford Street

The Roulette Cycle Co. was set up in 1890 by Frederick Kerby and Henry Hewitt. Kerby was born in Allesley in 1866, at that time a village just outside Coventry. After gaining experience in the thriving cycle industry, at the age of 24 he found suitable premises at Gosford Street, and began to manufacture cycles of his own in partnership with publican, Henry Hewitt. Some twenty years later, and well after many other cycle firms had experimented, Roulette began to make motorcycles powered by 2½hp, 292cc JAP engines, fitted to a specially developed frame that was hoped would be sold under license to other firms. The design was masterminded by Birmingham-born Fred T. Robb, which incorporated duplex tubes bolted together, so if any were damaged they could easily be replaced. Larger models were soon offered using Villiers engines, but the outbreak of the First World War cut short the potential of this enterprising

Above: A neat looking Roulette of 1911. As a business they lasted until 1919. (Mortons Media)

Right: Detail of the 1911 Roulette's JAP engine. (Mortons Media)

company, concentrating solely on cycles until 1919. The principle of Robb's frame design though would later be taken up by Francis-Barnett.

ROVER, 1898–1927 (1877–1945)

The Rover Cycle Co. Ltd, Meteor Works, West Orchard
The Rover Motor Co. Ltd, New Meteor Works, Rover Road (formerly Garfield Road)

The Rover concern was one of the very first to be established as pure cycle manufacturers in Coventry, and certainly one of the most significant to do so. James Starley (b. 1830) had been involved with the Coventry cycle industry from the very beginning along with the likes of Turner, Hillman and Singer. His early pioneering work was later taken up by his nephew, John Kemp Starley (b. 1855), and in 1877, J.K. established the firm of Starley & Sutton with William Sutton, building 'Ordinary' cycles as well as tricycles at West Orchard. By 1885 Starley used the 'Rover' name for the very first time with the invention of his Rover safety bicycle. This revolutionary design allowed cycling to become accessible to millions more people worldwide, and this style of bicycle is still, by-and-large, the one in use today. In 1888, Starley & Sutton experimented with motorised transport for the first time with an electric car, but because of British restrictions and a general lack of interest, this type of developmental work was unfortunately cut short. In 1896, the company became the Rover Cycle Co. Ltd under Harry Smith (b. 1863) as Managing Director, moving into new and larger premises at Garfield Road, and two years later began developing their first experimental motorcycles. At this time, Smith also lured Designer Edmund Lewis away from the Daimler Co. and appointed Londoner Ernest Courtis as Chief Tester. It wasn't until 1903 however that Rover manufactured motorcycles for general sale, these being Lewis-designed 2¼hp machines, increased to 3hp the following year. At the same time, Rover were becoming more prominent in motorcar manufacture, so although continuing on a limited scale, motorcycles took a back seat over the next few years. In 1910, Yorkshireman John E. Greenwood (b. 1873) had been placed on Rover's books and designed a 3½hp belt-driven machine with a rear-mounted Bosch magneto and B&B carburettor, and this sold well up to the outbreak of war. At this time, George Ravenhall (later of R&H) was in position at Rover as Works Manager. After the war came a 654cc JAP V-Twin range with a TT model by 1921, and by 1923 the twin was replaced by a lightweight machine powered by a 249cc engine. By now, the company had a very strong foothold in car production, so once again they eased off their motorcycle involvement, ceasing all manufacture in 1927.

A Rover motorcycle of the 1920s. Their first production models were offered in 1898. (Coventry Transport Museum)

A Rover advertisment for 1925. By 1927 all motorcycle production had ceased in order to concentrate on cars. (Coventry Transport Museum)

Under new Managing Directors Colonel Frank Searle and Jack Starley, and General Manager Spencer Wilks, Rover successfully continued car production at the Meteor Works until 1940 when much of the factory was destroyed by air-raid bombings. Operations picked up once again on a minimal scale while new works were developed in Solihull, but by 1945, Rover had moved out of Coventry altogether after some sixty-eight years of activity.

ROYAL EAGLE, 1901–1910 (1890–1945)

The Coventry Eagle Cycle & Motor Co., Lincoln Street, 201 Foleshill Road, & Stoney Stanton Road, Foleshill

In 1901, the Coventry Eagle Co. began selling their machines under the 'Royal Eagle' name. This was often practiced in business to suit the marketing needs of the overseas market. The company's 1902 catalogue featured a Royal Eagle motor-bicycle fitted with a 1½hp Minerva engine priced at £45. The supporting information reads:

> Of the various types of motor bicycles now on the market, the 'Royal Eagle' is undoubtedly one of the most elegant and efficient yet introduced. The motor is of the 'Minerva' type, and has long been proved to be eminently satisfactory in every particular. We anticipate a considerable demand for this motor, as we believe it is gaining in public favour every day. The one here shown embodies all the very latest and most up-to-date improvements, and intending motorcyclists cannot possibly do better than invest in a Royal Eagle.

This marque lasted until 1910, when the Mayo family opted to use the Coventry Eagle from then on.
(See also Coventry Eagle.)

RUDGE, 1910–1940 (1869–1940)

Rudge-Whitworth Ltd, Crow Lane & 34 Spon Street

Rudge cycles were first built in Wolverhampton by pub landlord Dan Rudge as early as 1869. When he died in 1880, his widow sold the business to Coventry solicitor and entrepreneur, George Woodcock, who had already acquired the cycle firms of Haynes & Jefferis and Smith & Starley. Before long, Woodcock began selling cycles under D. Rudge & Co. at Crow Lane, but soon after changed the firm's name to the Rudge Cycle Co., and as Managing Director he brought in a number of personnel, some of whom would prove to become significant in the British cycle and motor industries. These included Charles Vernon Pugh as Director, William H. Nelson as Works Manager, Victor A. Holroyd as Sales Manager, Sidney Smith as Accountant, and none other than Harry J. Lawson as Sales Manager. In 1894, the company merged with the Whitworth Cycle Co. of Birmingham to become Rudge-Whitworth Ltd, and by 1897, they were producing some 25,000 cycles a year at their enlarged Spon Street Works. Considering that Rudge-Whitworth quickly became major players in the cycle industry, it wasn't until 1910 that they added motorcycles to their output, many years after some of their local rivals had already done so. Their first motorcycle was fitted with a 3½hp engine with overhead inlet-valve and of chain-drive to the camshaft and magneto. In 1911 the company introduced their own variable gear to the machine, and a year later came their 'Rudge Multi' model, which gained many victories over the following years on the national racing circuit. After the war, Rudge concentrated again on targeting racing successes on machines then modified and sold for standard road use. These included the 1921 499cc 'TT', the 'Roadster Multi' and the 999cc V-Twin. On 2 July 1928, Rudge Sales Agent Stanley Glanfield embarked on a world tour on his Coventry-built 499cc Rudge motorcycle combination. The journey was to take him just eight

The great Rudge-Whitworth Works once towered over much of central Coventry. (Coventry Transport Museum)

A Rudge outing under the Coat of Arms Bridge in Coventry. (Coventry Transport Museum)

months – covering 18,000 miles, passing through some sixteen countries and crossing four continents. This event ultimately raised the company's profile and increased sales due to the machines proven reliability. On Glanfield's return, he reported stories about the new sport of 'Dirt Track' racing in Australia, which soon took off in England largely down to Glanfield's own promotional work. Rudge were quick to get involved and released a 499cc Speedway model of their own which saw many successes at new tracks around the country. 1928 also saw works rider Graham Walker winning the Ulster Grand Prix, which brought about the release of the Rudge 'Ulster' the very next year. Successes continued into the 1930s with victories for Tyrell Smith, Jimmy Simpson and Wal Handley at the Isle of Man TT, yet the company began to find the financial side of racing more and more draining until pulling out altogether in 1935. The next few years were difficult ones for the Rudge Co., which sadly fell into liquidation. In 1940 it was surprisingly purchased by The Gramophone Co., part of the EMI group. All business was moved to their factory at Hayes where they began making Rudge 'Autocycles', but this was shortlived.

(See also Lawson.)

Above: The Rudge-Whitworth finishing shop. Note the two female workers on the right. (Coventry Transport Museum)

Right: The Rudge-Whitworth Ulster was introduced in 1929. (Coventry Transport Museum)

SAXEL, 1923–1927 (1920–1939)

Saxelby's Ltd, Sax Works, 29 Much Park Street

The firm of Saxelby's Ltd was established at Sax Works on Much Park Street around 1920. The company was founded by Fred A. Saxelby (b. 1885) of Leicester, a graduate Mechanical Engineer and Draughtsman. Often known as Saxelby's Accessories, they began as a motor accessories company also offering components for the trade under their own name. In 1923 they started to add motorcycles to their output with two early models powered by a 349cc Barr & Stroud engine, and the other, a lightweight 147cc Villiers. These motorcycles were sold under the 'Saxel' name, and were most probably assembled using frames and other parts from local suppliers. Not much is known of Saxelby's engineering work after 1927, yet ten years later, he and a Mr P.H. Jones were seen to be running a business called 'Saxess Chairs', makers of 'steel office chairs, stools and deck chairs' at the Sax Works address.

(See also Saxessories.)

Mr B. Raven of Coventry, pictured on his 3.5hp Rudge-Whitworth in 1921. (John Raven)

SAXESSORIES, 1923 (1920–1939)

Saxelby's Ltd, Sax Works, 29 Much Park Street

In 1923, Saxelby's also offered a motorcycle under the name of 'Saxessories'. This was really a very basic 'no thrills' belt-driven 247cc Villiers-powered model targeting the lower end of the market, and claimed by the company to weigh just 150lbs. Considering the machine was only on offer inside a year then one can assume that it was not too well received. It is not known exactly when the company ceased to concern themselves with engineering but they are still seen in the 1926/27 *Coventry Spennell Directory* listed under 'Motorcycle Manufacturers', and by 1939, 'Cycle Agents'.
(See also Saxel.)

SERVICE, 1911–1913

Wartnaby & Draper, 21 Coundon Road, Coundon

Service was another company based in London who outsourced the assembly of their motorcycles to other firms. Known as Service & Colonial Ltd, they had an address at 292 High Holborn and from 1911–1913 arranged for motorcycles built by Wartnaby & Draper of Coventry to be transferred and sold under the Service name. These were said to be machines fitted with JAP engines with 'forced lubrication'. During the same period, Wartnaby & Draper sold their own machines under the W.D. marque. There appears to be further links with Service, W.D. and the Birmingham company Connaught, who ran from 1913–1929, the details of which are unclear.
(See also W.D.)

SINGER, 1900–1921 (1874–1970)

Singer & Co. Ltd, 50–54 Canterbury Street, Hillfields
Singer Motor Co. Ltd, 50–54 Canterbury Street, Hillfields

George Singer, the son of a Farm Bailiff, was born in Kingston, Dorset in January 1847. On leaving school he gained an apprenticeship at the Marine Engineers John Penn & Sons of Lewisham before moving to Coventry in 1869. Along with the likes of Hillman, Bayliss

Right: George Singer first worked for the Coventry Machinists Co. before going into partnership. (Coventry Transport Museum)

Below: Singer made a fortune in Coventry and had his own house, Coundon Court built in 1891. (Richard Hoare)

The Singer Motor-Wheel, the design of which was purchased from Edwin Perks and Frank Birch. (Coventry Transport Museum)

and Herbert, Singer was one of the first men to be employed at the Coventry Machinists Co. under Josiah Turner and James Starley. In 1873 he resigned his position of Foreman and became Manager for Charles D. Roberts Paragon Cycle Co. By 1874, he had married Elizabeth Stringer and in partnership with brother-in-law James Charles Stringer, founded his own cycle company at Leicester Street building 'Challenge' cycles. Two years later they moved to a purpose-built factory at Canterbury Street designed by architect Charles Harry Quick. However, these works were found to be insufficient in size, so new buildings were extended at the rear over a disused ice-rink. By 1883, the reputation of the company had grown, becoming one of the largest cycle firms in the country, supplying cycles to many people of note, including the Queen of Portugal. Because of such success, more production space was needed so Singer & Co. acquired additional buildings once used by the celebrated craftsman and metal worker Francis Skidmore, at Alma Street. In the same year, the Singer workforce founded the city's first football team as Singers FC, which later became Coventry City Football Club in 1889. In 1890, Singer commissioned Charles Gray Hill to build him and his wife a large house on the outskirts of Coventry, the result of which was Coundon Court, completed in 1891 in rural Coundon, and neighbouring one of the company's Directors, A.E. Jagger. In 1899, Edwin Perks and Frank Birch unveiled their 'Motor-Wheel' design, and this was taken up by Singer the following year in the form of a motorized tricycle and bicycle, along with the services of Perks & Birch. At around this time, George Ernest Singer junior joined the business, and under the expertise of Herbert Duret and Clifford Ingall, the Singer Co. released a range of 2hp and 3hp models fitted with upright engines of belt and chain drive, as well as a V-Twin tricar. By 1910, they introduced the 'Moto-Velo' lightweight motorcycle, powered by a 1¼hp 211cc Dufaux engine, and the next year saw a 499cc 3½hp version added, which was then exhibited at the 1911 Cycle, Motor Cycle and Accessories Exhibition at Olympia. The same year saw Singer produce a side-valve 499cc racing machine that

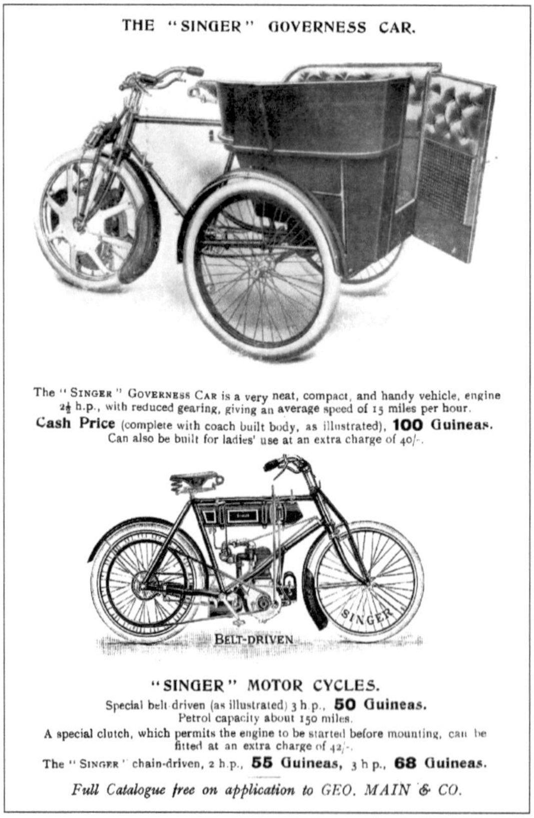

The Singer Co. tried to appeal to a broad audience through their product sales. (Coventry Transport Museum)

was ridden by G.E. Stanley with marginal success at Brooklands, but in the Senior event at the Isle of Man TT, Stanley completed the course in a disappointing 19th place. As well as cycles and motorcycles, Singer & Co. Ltd had been experimenting with motorcars from 1905, and this is where the company ultimately concentrated its development until 1970, ceasing the production of motorcycles around 1921. George Singer himself retired around 1901, and sadly died in 1909 following an apoplectic seizure at the dinner table of his Coundon Court home. He is buried in a large grave at London Road cemetery. Coundon Court and its grounds were modernized and became a school in 1953.
(See also Perks & Birch.)

SMITH & MOLESWORTH
(See Alert.)

SPARK, 1922–1923
Sparkbrook Manufacturing Co. Ltd, 72–74 Payne's Lane, Stoke

The 'Spark' name was used briefly by the Sparkbrook Co. from 1922 for a 247cc single-speed two-stroke Villiers belt-driven machine priced at £35. It had a single top-tube frame on which a rounded petrol tank was fixed. This was basically a stripped down version of the standard Sparkbrook model with a smaller engine, less refinements, and generally aimed at the lower end of the market. The marque was discontinued the following year, but the company produced touring models until 1926.
(See also Sparkbrook.)

SPARKBROOK, 1912–1926 (1883–1926)
Sparkbrook Manufacturing Co. Ltd, 72–74 Payne's Lane, Stoke

The name of this cycle firm has for many years caused confusion as to why a Coventry company should take a Birmingham name. The explanation evolves from the Birmingham small arms trade, when in 1872, the National Arms & Ammunition Co. were established at Montgomery Street, in the Sparkbrook suburb of Birmingham. By the end of the decade, the business was

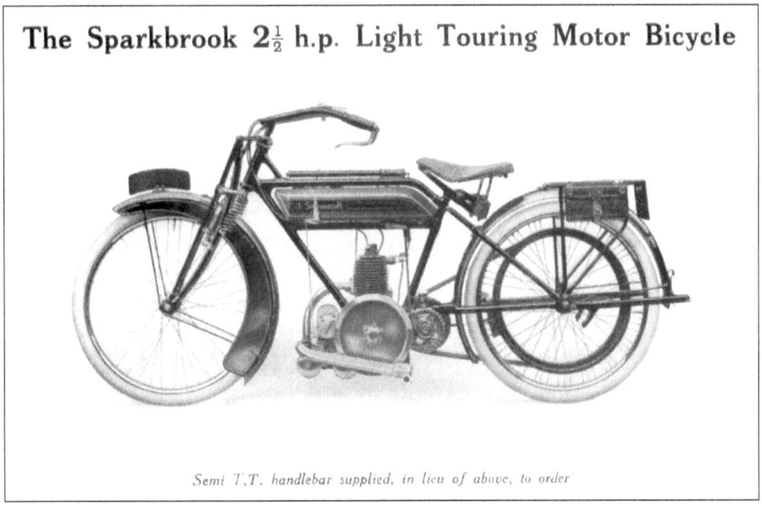

William Hillman purchased the Sparkbrook Co. in 1883. (Coventry Transport Museum)

experiencing low orders, so the management took the decision to begin the manufacture of cycles and tricycles in one part of the factory in the hope of generating additional income. This turned out to be a bad decision and within the year the receivers were brought in. The cycle side was salvaged by William Hillman, who transferred all equipment along with Works Manager Mr A.H.M. Driver to Much Park Street, Coventry, before moving to purpose-built works at Payne's Lane under the supervision of Cecil Wheeler. Much later, in 1912, the company began to experiment in the development of motorcycles, fitted with various size JAP motors, but it wasn't until 1914 that they made a serious start. With F.S. Mathews being employed as the new Works Manager, they announced the release of a 269cc Villiers two-stroke light touring machine, known as the 'Model A'. The outbreak of war slowed production somewhat but they were back in full swing by 1919, continuing with their Villiers touring range. In 1920 their sales catalogue stated: 'The Sparkbrook light motor cycle, since its introduction in 1914, has taken a place in the front rank of its class', and by 1923 the company was, 'specialising in lightweights of the 250cc and 350cc classes fitted with JAP, Villiers and Barr & Stroud engines'. Their final motorcycles came in 1926 when all production ended.
(See also Hillman, Revere, and Spark.)

STAFFORD, 1919–1921

Stafford Auto Scooters Ltd, Alvis Engineering Co., Birmingham Road (now Holyhead Road)

The Stafford Auto-Scooter was introduced in 1919 by T.G. John, later of Alvis Motor Co. fame. However, it failed to win over the market with its bizarre visual design, and was extremely impractical, having much of its engine weight above the front wheel. One of two sons, Thomas George John was born at Argyle Street in 1880 at Pembroke Dock in Wales. His father was employed at the HM Dockyard and Thomas and his brother Charles soon followed into the profession. By 1904 he was qualified as a Naval Architect winning two scholarships with the Royal College of Science. He rose quickly in his field and by 1915 moved to the Siddeley-Deasy Motor Car Co. in Coventry as Works Manager and Chief Engineer. In 1919 he purchased the American-owned company, Holley Brothers & Co. Ltd, renaming it T.G. John & Co. Ltd, for the 'sole manufacture of engines for land, sea and air'. In 1919, at a time when there was a great need for cheap motorised transport, he set his workforce of fifty to work on the Stafford 'Mobile Pup'. The frames were supplied by the Birmingham Guild, and powered by 140cc overhead valve engines on behalf of Stafford Auto Scooters Ltd of Coventry. Around 100 machines were said to have been built, one of which was taken to Scotland by Works Engineer George Tattersall, who won a race at Dunoon – effectively the first ever Alvis victory. T.G. John retired to his Kenilworth estate in 1944 and died two years later.

The original Alvis Works on Holyhead Road where the Stafford Auto Scooter was developed. (Coventry Transport Museum)

T.G. John, creator of the Stafford Auto Scooter and founder of the famous Alvis Motor Co. (Coventry Transport Museum)

STAN, 1919–1921

Stan Motor Co., Westwood Heath

The only address ever to be sourced for this company was Westwood Heath, Coventry. Today (2009) this area is adjacent to a business park and Warwick University, but in the early 1920s would have been nothing more than a rural village. Why an engineering firm would chose to situate itself some six miles outside the centre of Coventry is a mystery, yet in 1919 the Stan Motor Co. was founded there and began to produce lightweight motorcycles assembled from other outsourced parts. They were powered by 2¾hp two-stroke engines for a couple of years, before fading from records in 1921. Whether 'Stan' was the first or second name of the owner is unknown, typical of the lack of records that exist for such small, short-lived companies.

STANLEY, 1902 (1898–1902)

Stanley Bicycle and Motor Co. Ltd,
Days Lane & Payne's Lane, Stoke

This company was founded in 1898 at the Stanley Cycle Works at Days Lane. Its founder was thought to have been a Mr William Stanley, a 36-year-old Coventrian who had drawn years of experience in engineering from working in the cycle trade.

G.E. Stanley won many races for the Singer Co. (Coventry Transport Museum)

The motoring side may well have came from a Mr Frank Stanley, who can be seen working as a 'Motor Engineer' by 1901. Little is known about their motorcycles, except that they were of friction-drive to the rear wheel. The engine would probably have been a Belgian Minerva or Coventry-made MMC fitted to another manufacturer's frame. Their finished product must have been quite appealing, though, as the Stanley business was acquired by the Singer Motor Co. in 1902. Small companies such as Stanley could never compete with the likes of Singer, who were backed by major investors and shareholders. Chances are, though, that upon sale of the firm, the small Stanley workforce would have taken up positions offered to them by the Singer Co. Indeed, a Mr George Enoch Stanley was known to have won numerous races for Singer at Brooklands and the Isle of Man TT from 1911 onwards. Incidentally, George Stanley was the nephew of William Stanley, reported to be one of the co-founders of Singers FC, the original name of Coventry City Football Club.

(See also Singer.)

STAR, 1919–1921

New Star Co., Broad Lane, Tile Hill

The New Star Co. of Broad Lane, Coventry entered the motorcycle field in 1919 with a two-speed belt-driven machine powered by a 269cc Villiers engine. Although the company only appeared to be in operation for a couple of years, for some reason they also marketed their machines under the 'Coventry Star' and 'New Star' names. Starting a business after a world war was never going to be easy, and resulted in the company lasting just two years.

(See also Coventry Star, and New Star.)

The Starley family became world famous cycle makers. (Coventry Transport Museum)

STARLEY, 1903

Starley's Ltd, St John's Works
The Swift Motor Co. Ltd, 15 Cheylesmore, & Quinton Works, Parkside

William Starley was a direct family member of both James Starley, known as the 'Father of the Cycle Industry', and J.K. Starley, the inventor of the Rover safety bicycle. The 1901 census shows two men by this name who are most likely father and son: William Starley aged 42 of Lewisham, working in Coventry as a 'Cycle Manufacturer', and William A. Starley aged 24 of Coventry, also working in the city as a 'Cycle Manufacturer'. The Starley motor-bicycle was built in 1903 under the company of Starley's Ltd, based at St John's Works, and they were the

J.F. Starley, son of William Starley, seated on his father's motor-bicycle. (Coventry Transport Museum)

only firm that year to exhibit a worm-driven single track machine. In his 1961 book *Veteran and Vintage Motorcycles*, James Sheldon states:

> Mr W. Starley, in association with Messer's Accles and De Veulle, used two front down tubes and a vertical engine. He set his engine across the frame with worm-drive to the bottom bracket via a two speed gear and clutch, with final drive by chain, and the machine was produced by the Swift Cycle Co. at Coventry.

To support this, Harold Connolly adds in his *Motorcycle Story 1875–1905* (1962):

> Starley was famous in the racing bicycle days, and was the inventor of the differential gear for use on racing tricycles. This 1903 machine is notable for its very original ideas. It was one of the first unit construction power units, with the horizontal engine across the frame and a two-speed gear through a worm drive to the pedal crank-case, thence by slow speed chain to the rear wheel.

(See also Accles, Swift and Rover.)

SWIFT, 1898–1915 (1868–1955)

The Swift Motor Co. Ltd, 15 Cheylesmore, & Quinton Works, Parkside

The Swift name is one that can not only lay claim to being associated with the first cycle manufacturers in Coventry, but also in Britain, directly descending from Starley & Turners Coventry Machinists Co., which began making velocipedes in 1868. In 1897, Birmingham-based Dunlop took over the Coventry Machinists with a principal capital of £300,000, re-establishing the business as the Swift Cycle Co. Ltd on their original Cheylesmore site. Lord Randolph Churchill was appointed Chairman of this new concern, while Irish brothers Harvey and Arthur Du Cros were placed as Directors. Closely connected to the Ariel firm of Birmingham, Swift's first motorised machine took the form of a well-built De Dion Bouton type tricycle powered by a 1¾hp engine mounted ahead of the rear axle. In 1904, they began making a motorcycle built under license from William Starley, the design of which they continued with until 1910. At this time they introduced their 'Swift-Ariel' machine, powered by a 3½hp engine, and the following year saw them use White & Poppe power units for their Touring and TT models. The company's concentration on car production intensified and by 1913 they released a 3½hp water-cooled cycle-car. This transition signified Swift's future intentions, seeing all motorcycle manufacture stop by 1915. Like many other related Coventry companies, the motorcar took preference with management and shareholders. Swift were no exception and successfully manufactured cars in Coventry until 1931, but sold bicycles at Balsall Heath until 1955.

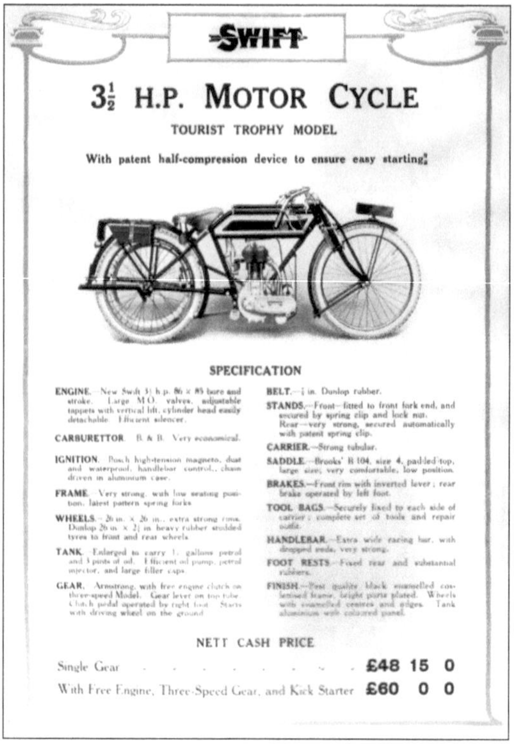

The Swift Tourist Trophy model of 1913. (Coventry Transport Museum)

THREE SPIRES, 1931–1932

Coventry Bicycles Ltd, Barbury & Downes, Osborne Road, Earlsdon

A fitting Coventry name, from 1931 Coventry Bicycles Ltd introduced the 'Three Spires' motorcycle. This was a trademark previously used by the company in the production of cycles, but was also briefly sold as a 'Petro-cycle' using a 147cc Villiers Junior power unit and a two-speed Albion gearbox. At the rear of all models came a round toolbox as standard. At slightly more cost, the owner could also opt for an engine cover, Villiers lighting and a rear stand, all for £18.90, with a back-pedalling brake as an additional extra. The term 'Three Spires' was in reference to the three spires of Coventry which once dominated the skyline, and fortunately, all still remain.

(See also Coventry B&D, Coventry B&S, and Wee McGregor.)

A Three Spires motorcycle of 1932 made by Coventry Bicycles Ltd. (Mortons Media)

TIPPEN, 1948–1956 (1935–1976)

Frank Tippen & Sons Ltd, Shakespeare Street, Stoke Heath

Frank Tippen started his first business in 1935 at Shakespeare Street making variable gears for machine drives under the name of 'Heterospeed'. In 1948 he developed a motorised 'Invalid Chair' powered by a small two-stroke engine. It was manufactured with great success until 1956, when the AC 'Invacar' was favoured. *Coventry Produces* (1950) states, 'A further example of the wide variety of the city's products, is the "Coventry" Motor Tricycle Invalid Chair, designed and manufactured to the Ministry of Pensions' specification by Frank Tippen & Sons Ltd. This Firm also produces variable speed gears for industrial purposes'. After 1956, Tippen & Sons adapted their products to keep up to date with the changing market, creating the 'Delta' by 1966 to rival the AC Invacar. Unfortunately the popularity of the Invacar was too great, and Tippen reverted to the manufacture of variable gears until closure in 1976.

TOWNEND, 1901–1904 (1871–1905)

New Townend Bros Ltd, 83 Gosford Street & Payne's Lane, Stoke

The Townend Brothers were founded as cycle manufacturers as far back as 1871, not too long after Coventry had first established connections with the industry. The company was started by George Townend, initially at Wellington Street, then Lower Ford Street before settling at Far Gosford Street. Townend was born in 1829 in Haworth in Yorkshire, and his cycle business soon became a family affair, with son Frank taking over the reigns as Manager at the turn of the century. Renamed the New Townend Bros Ltd, the company began to sell cycles under the 'Wellington Harrier' name. Frank was also born in Haworth, in 1861, which indicates that the family did not make the move to Coventry until after this date, and probably not until after 1868, when the Coventry Machinists Co. constructed the first bicycle in the city. Frank Townend then in turn brought in his own sons to work for the firm, Coventry-born Frank and

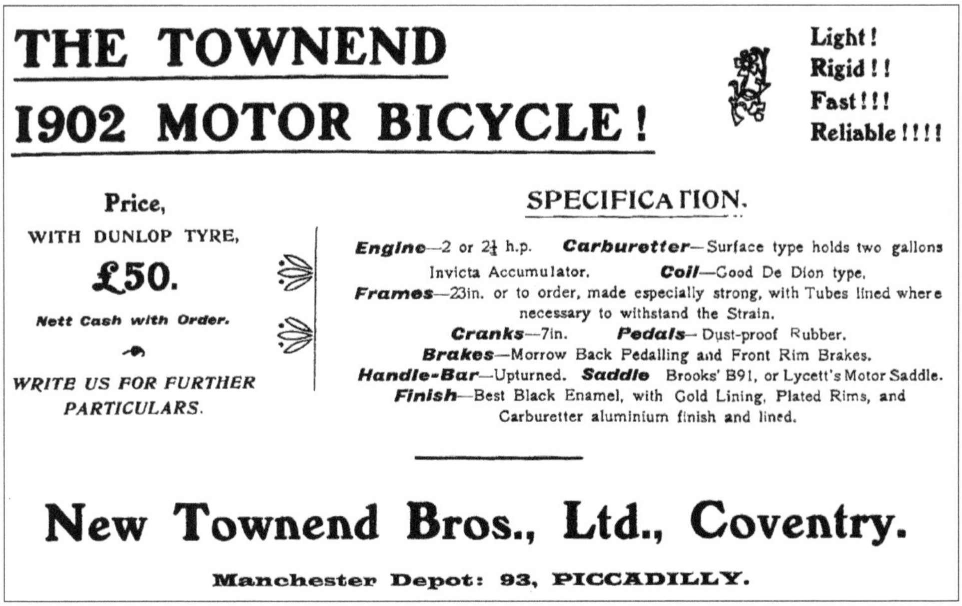

The Townend brothers made their first motor-bicycles in 1901; the company began making cycles thirty years earlier. (Coventry Transport Museum)

Ernest, seen to be working as 'Cycle Fitters' by 1901. In the same year the company began to experiment with motorcycles assembled from various parts fitted to their own frames. Said to be 'Light, rigid, fast and reliable', these machines were offered with a 2hp and 2¼hp engine and finished in 'Best black enamel, with gold lining, plated rims, and carburettor aluminum finish and lined'. Unfortunately the firm was seen to go into voluntary liquidation in late 1902 yet the actual venture somehow lasted until around 1904. By 1905 the company were reformed as Townend & Co. at Hearsall Lane under the ownership of Frank Townend, but this is where the trail runs dry.

TRIUMPH, 1902–1940 & 1942–1982 (1886–1982)

Triumph Cycle Co. Ltd, Much Park Street, Priory Street & Dale Street
Triumph Engineering Co. Ltd (1936), Meriden Works, Allesley

One of the truly great names of the industry, Triumph, are the only company to feature in this compilation that still exist at the time of writing (2008) as manufacturers of motorcycles, albeit now outside Coventry. Their start began in 1886 when Siegfried Bettmann began selling British-made bicycles under the Triumph name and then selling them abroad. Bettmann was born in Germany in 1863, and moved to England in 1883, later establishing Bettmann & Co. in London as exporters of cycles. By 1886, Bettmann took the decision to manufacture his own cycles. He changed the firm's name to the Triumph Cycle Co. Ltd and was joined by Mauritz Johann Schulte (b. 1858), a friend and fellow German who had recently trained at William Andrews' cycle factory in Birmingham, the source of their previous export business. At this time, Coventry was the centre of cycle production, so Bettmann and Schulte wasted little time in moving there, finding suitable premises to rent at Much Park Street, and the company soon employed some 100 men. By 1894 Triumph had moved to a much larger factory at Priory Street, just a stone's throw from their former works. They were keen to get involved in the development of motorised transport that had already been active in Belgium, France and Germany, but had now begun to be tried and tested in Coventry. In 1895 Schulte had a German-built Hildebrand-Wolfmuller 2½hp motorcycle shipped to Coventry and studied its make-up in great detail. This was the

The great Triumph Works at Priory Street, first built in 1894 and later extended. (Coventry Transport Museum)

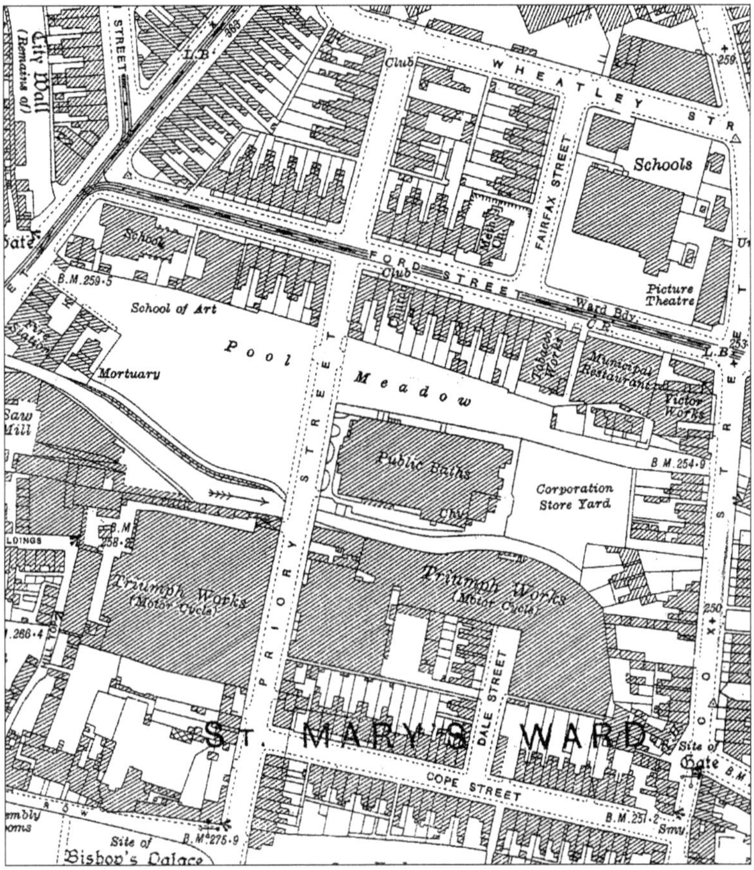

The Triumph Works as recorded in 1925. Today the new Cathedral and Coventry University take its place. (Ordnance Survey)

world's first motorcycle to be produced and sold commercially and it created quite a stir in the city. Although at this point Triumph were arguably the largest cycle firm in the country, they also quietly experimented in motorcycle production, yet waited patiently until they were satisfied with a quality product. This came about in 1902 with the release of a suitably modified bicycle frame fitted with a 2¼hp Minerva engine, the overall finish of which was of very high quality, yet unreliable. At this time the company were selling around 300 motorcycles each year.

Joined in 1890 by Londoner Charles Hathaway (b. 1865), the company had developed their own 363cc engine by 1905. By 1906 Triumph were selling over 500 machines a year, 1,000 in 1907, 2,000 in 1908 and around 3,000 in 1909. Hathaway was a gifted Design Engineer and motorcyclist and was behind the 3hp single-cylinder model – with a top speed of 45mph, and indeed most of the company's early engineering development. Also representing Triumph in competitions was Company Secretary Robert Ayton (b. 1871), and Frank Hulbert, who seemingly finished in the top three at most of the country's events. Triumph continued much in the same vein with their original 1905 engine, but steadily increased its capacity from 363cc to 550cc by the outbreak of the First World War, which it remained by and large until well into the 1920s. Unlike many companies that folded, Triumph had profited between the years 1914 and 1918 having won a huge contract from the War Office to supply 30,000 motorcycles for service. These machines were labelled 'Trusty Triumphs' by the soldiers that used them because of their reliability in variable conditions, and as a result, Triumph entered into the 1920s with great confidence. The only downside was the departure of Schulte, who left after a disagreement with Bettmann. Schulte wanted to cease the manufacture of bicycles and instead focus future production on cars, but Bettmann thought otherwise, and this ultimately brought an end to their long friendship. In Schulte's place, Bettmann brought in Lieutenant-Colonel Claude Vivian Holbrook, who had been influential in Triumph's previous war contracts, and Works Manager J.J. Philips. In 1922, they unveiled their 499cc 'Riccy' machine designed by Harry Ricardo, and in a blow to Schulte, the following year, built their first motorcar fitted with a Ricardo-designed engine. By 1923, Triumph was selling between 300 and 400 motorcycles per week, and sometimes more. 1924 saw the release of the 'Model P', a 500cc side-valve machine that was priced at just £14 17*s* 6*d*, much lower than any other similar manufactured motorcycle on the market. However, in the absence of Schulte, Triumph steadily let their standards drop and cut many corners in the production of the Model P. This machine took a beating in the media and the company were quick to make the necessary upgrades in the production of the Mark II, which, fortunately for them, won back the public's approval. The end of the 1920s saw the traditional flat tank replaced by the saddle tank, and the beginning of the 1930s marked a tough era for the industry during difficult economic times. Lloyd's Bank Official Receiver Mr Graham was eventually called in to try to salvage the company, and it was during this time that Siegfried Bettmann parted company with Triumph. The results of Graham's recommendations saw Ariel's Jack Sangster effectively save the company by taking on Triumph's manufacturing rights, establishing the Triumph Engineering Co. Sangster soon drafted in Ariel designers Val Page and Edward Turner, Turner being made Chief Designer and Managing Director by 1935. Two years later, the revolutionary 500cc 'Speed Twin' was launched at the 1937 Motorcycle Show at £75, changing the way all motorcycles would be built from then on.

On the night of 14 November 1940, Triumph's Priory Street Works were all but completely destroyed along with much of central Coventry during the Blitz. Turner quickly found a disused factory at Warwick to commence limited production, which lasted for two years until a brand new Triumph facility was opened up at Meriden, north-west of Coventry. The first 1942 models were 350cc ohv single-cylinder W.D. machines, supported by the Speed Twin, the 3T and the Tiger 100. After the war, Ernie Lyons won the 1946 Manx Grand Prix on a Tiger 100 and sales were booming, not only in Britain but also on foreign shores, particularly in America. The 1950s and '60s saw production concentrate heavily on the American market, with the introduction of the 650cc Thunderbird, a continuation of the Tiger range, and the Bonneville 120 by 1959. In 1960, Triumph introduced the 650cc Trophy and the 200cc Tiger Cub, and gave the Thunderbird a face-lift to fit in with the times. They also recognised that the introduction of Italian Scooters were having an impact on sales so released their own in the form of the 100cc T10, but although marginally successful, it could not compete with the appeal of the Vespa or Lambretta models. Triumph had also been concentrating on record attempts in

A Triumph Speed Twin of 1949. The Speed Twin was first designed by Edward Turner in 1937 and revolutionised the motorcycle world. (Coventry Transport Museum)

Triumph's first commercial motorcycle of 1902. (Coventry Transport Museum)

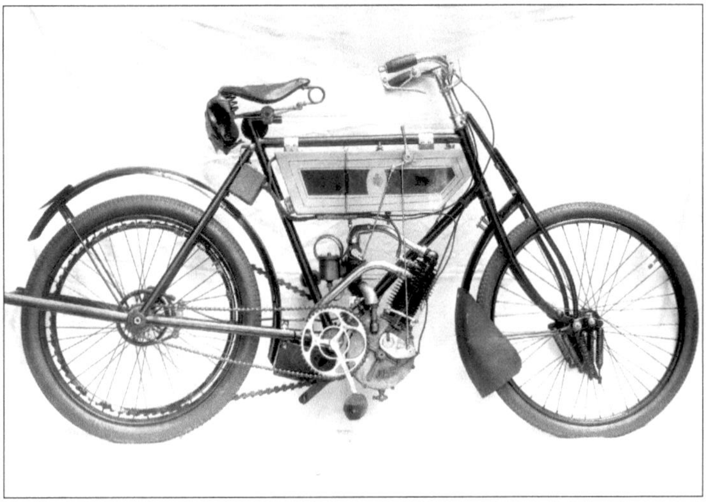

A 1907 Triumph model as developed by Charles Hathaway. (Coventry Transport Museum)

the hope of increasing sales, and in 1962, they succeeded when American Bill Johnson piloted a Bonneville-powered streamliner to a new world record of 224.57mph. In 1966 they struck gold again, when Bob Leppan recorded a two-way average speed of 245.6mph in America. By now however, Japan had began to take a stronghold on the international market and became a growing threat to Britain's overall motorcycle industry. Slowly but surely, Honda, Suzuki, Yamaha and Kawasaki made a greater impact in the European market, able to produce quality machines at cheaper prices, and this began to take its toll on Triumph. The company had already become part of BSA through Jack Sangster's ties in 1951, yet when he retired in 1960, he left the company in a very healthy state, announcing record profits of £3,500,000. Edward Turner retired as Managing Director in 1964 when sales were still relatively good, but by 1971, BSA announced a massive overall loss of £8,500,000. Two years later, Triumph merged with Norton-Villiers to establish NVT, but plans to move production to Small Heath, Birmingham ignited a workers 'sit-in'. This action lasted nearly two years and resulted in the creation of an employer's co-operative, yet pride was maintained with the re-introduction of the 'Bonneville' model, and in 1977, the iconic 'Jubilee' Bonneville. Despite all attempts to get the company back on track, it was too little too late and by 1982 all production was ceased and the factory sold, being completely demolished by the summer of the following year. However,

A Triumph Speed Twin of 1957, twenty years after its conception. (Coventry Transport Museum)

The Triumph Bonneville 1977 Jubilee 750cc – built during uncertain times at Meriden. (Coventry Transport Museum)

this was not the end of the Triumph name. Like Sangster had done half a decade before, in 1985, local businessman John Bloor bought the manufacturing rights to the company and set about building a new manufacturing facility in Hinckley, Leicestershire, completed in 1988. Finally, in 1990, production resumed with the release of the Trident, Trophy and Daytona models, and by the new millennium, Triumph had once again re-established themselves as brand contenders around the world.

(See also Gloria.)

Siegfried Bettmann (1863–1951)

Siegfried Bettmann was born in the Bavarian Alps of Germany on 18 April 1863. His father was 59-year-old Meyer Bettmann, a timber merchant who, by the time he married Siegfried's mother, Sophie Weil, had already been married twice before and fathered three children. Meyer and Sophie had a further nine children: five boys and four girls.

After being educated in Modern Classics in Nuremberg, Siegfried first joined the Army for a year at the age of 15. On completion he moved to Frankfurt and became apprentice for

Above: Bettmann and wife Millie pictured outside their home with a family friend. (Coventry Transport Museum)

Right: Siegfried Bettmann as Mayor in 1913. (Coventry Transport Museum)

the firm of Otto Meyer & Hamburg. In 1881 he relocated to Antwerp, Belgium and worked for Souheur & Neizest before once again moving, this time to Paris to work for a newspaper editor named Frison.

In the October 1883, at the relatively young age of 20, Bettmann moved to London in the hope of seeking his fortune along with a friend named Siegfried Dunkelsbuhler. For a brief period, Bettmann first moved into the Station Hotel at Holborn Viaduct, before finding less expensive accommodation at Church Road, Islington for 21*s* per week.

It was on his first night there that he became acquainted with the 25-year-old Mauritz Johann Schulte of Meppen, Germany, who had also just moved to London after spending seven years in Holland. They soon became loyal friends, supporting each other while both applying for work. Bettmann later gained employment at Kelly & Co., compiling Post Office and foreign directories for publication, and Schulte at the office of Paul Metz, Wholesale Ironmonger.

In the evenings they spent much of their time playing cards and learning Spanish. After about six months, both found work elsewhere, Bettmann for the White Sewing Machine Co. under American George Sawyer as Foreign Correspondent and Translator, and Schulte as a Foreign Salesman of chinaware and pottery.

In 1885, the White Sewing Machine Co. hit hard times, and Bettmann was laid off. Having gained experience of commercial travel, he decided to start his own business. So as S. Bettmann & Co. at offices at 9 Coleman Street, London, he began marketing German-built Biesolt & Locke sewing machines in Britain while marketing British bicycles abroad, chiefly with machines made by Hillman, Herbert & Cooper of Coventry. Unfortunately, business was slow and he was fortunate to take back his old position at White's while still managing his new venture in the hope that things would pick up.

In the November of 1886, Mauritz Schulte offered to join Bettmann as partner with a combined capital of £500 with the intention of making their own cycles under the 'Triumph' name. At this point Schulte had made a business arrangement with Birmingham

Elm Bank; the Bettmann's Stoke Green residence. (Coventry Transport Museum)

Cycle Manufacturer William Andrews to produce cycles to his design for sale overseas. While Bettmann was still working abroad, Schulte spent two months under Andrew's supervision to gain some mechanical experience to assist in their new venture. Again progress was slow and they decided that they would have to become genuine manufacturers in order to be taken seriously, and so were backed by Bettmann's ex-employer and adviser, George Sawyer, who became a principal shareholder and Chairman in the new business, Triumph Cycle Co. Ltd.

Schulte first visited Coventry, the birthplace of the British Cycle Industry, in 1889 to source a suitable workspace, and the following year found premises to rent at Earls Court, Much Park Street. This new venture was known to have been supported financially by both Bettmann and Schulte's relatives, plus Rowley B. Turner, Phillip Schloss, and two Coventry businessmen – Coventry watchmaker Alfred Fridlander, and A.S. Tomson.

Joined by new employees Edgar Hayes and Charles Hathaway, in July 1890, Schulte appointed John Woof, a Coventry carpenter and all began to fit out the new works, and soon after, full production began.

Having both lived in London for many years, Bettmann and Schulte found it difficult to adjust to working and living in a small provincial town. They first found lodgings under Mr and Mrs Baum at Barras Lane, a row of houses known locally as 'Bankrupt Terrace', an unfortunate name given that they were both in search of success. Yet, in 1894 Bettmann and Schulte moved the company to new purpose-built works at Priory Street, where they progressively became one of the largest employers in the city.

Meanwhile, on a social visit to friend Arthur Bones, a Chemist on High Street one afternoon, Bettmann was introduced to the proprietor's sister-in-law, Annie Meyrick, known as Millie. On 31 July 1895, Siegfried Bettmann married 30-year-old Millie at Shifnal in Shropshire and they both moved to a large house named Elm Bank at 9 North Avenue in the desirable Stoke Park area of Coventry. It was also about this time that Bettmann became a British Citizen.

Under the expert guidance of Works Manager Charles Hathaway, Triumph began to develop motorcycles to add to their cycle output and sold their first in 1902, steadily building up a reputation for producing machines of great quality. At around the same time, Bettmann became a local Freemason, a Justice of the Peace, and member of the City Council as a Liberal.

In 1913, he succeeded William Wyley to become Mayor of Coventry, the first non-British-born subject to do so. By this time, he had been a resident of the city for some twenty-four years and had employed thousands of people at the Triumph Co., and thus was a well-respected

Alderman George Hodgkinson and Siegfried Bettmann look on at Millie Bettmann's memorial at Canley Crematorium. (Coventry Transport Museum)

member of the community despite his foreign roots. But in August 1914, Britain declared war against Germany, and suddenly Bettmann found himself being literally 'sent to Coventry'. Caught up in a wave of anti-German hysteria, he was ostracised from many circles, including his removal from the board of the Standard Motor Co.

In later years he wrote:

> … my position became more untenable from day to day. I do not know which of the two burdens is heavier: to be shunned by erstwhile friends or to be openly persecuted by people who cannot possibly have a grudge against you except that of having an honoured name and being born on foreign soil.

Although shunned by many he once considered as friends and business associates, as Mayor for a second term, Bettmann continued to support Britain during the war, supplying 30,000 Model 'H' motorcycles for military duty as well as arranging for Belgian refugees to be housed at Whitley Abbey and being an active supporter of the British Red Cross Society. Despite such obvious support, he was still subjected to personal attacks by a small yet influential minority, and by November 1914 was forced to resign as Mayor. Undeterred, almost immediately he established the Annie Bettmann Foundation to support local men and women aged between 18 and 40 in starting up their own business, with special consideration towards ex-servicemen.

The following years were the most difficult for Bettmann, as he struggled to manage a business while under constant scrutiny from a large proportion of his staff and fellow peers. 1917 also saw the thirty-two-year partnership end between Bettmann and Schulte following too many differences of opinion.

At the conclusion of war, Triumph had lost sixty-six men on the battlefield. In honour of this, in March 1921, Bettmann commissioned a Triumph memorial at London Road cemetery for these ex-servicemen. Bettmann felt a great sense of loss for his former workers and made a touching speech in their memory, comparing their bravery to 'the heroic fight of Leonidas', the King of Spartas.

By this time he was being steadily invited to regain public status by those who had not long ago turned their backs on him. This he duly did by rejoining the board at Standard, but by now he was slowly winding down at Triumph, appointing Captain Claude Vincent Holbrook as Schulte's successor, and ultimately his own. Holbrook initiated the making of cars at Priory Street in 1923, but soon sought to produce sportier models, which drained much of

Triumphs recourses through investment and time. Here began a downward spiral of financial mismanagement which placed the company in a desperate state, and by 1932 Bettmann, downtrodden and with regret at appointing Holbrook, decided to retire.

By 1935, Triumph, under the miss-judged leadership of Holbrook, had collapsed. With a quickly formed consortium, Bettmann purchased Triumph's cycle business and formed Coventry Bicycles Ltd. The motorcycle side was fortunately saved by Jack Sangster of Birmingham-based Ariel, retaining full production in Coventry. Sangster then convinced Bettmann to rejoin as Chairman to which he later agreed, much to the embarrassment of Holbrook and causing a stir in the motoring press.

After stability was re-established at Triumph, with war once again looming against his native Germany, Bettmann, now in his 70s, decided to all but retire from any active involvement in Coventry's transport industry.

His final years were spent with his wife, travelling, reading and writing, and he kept a constant eye on the world politics, maintaining strong views. Millie Bettmann died on 17 February 1941 at the age of 76. Siegfried Bettmann died in 1951 at the grand age of 88 and is rested in Canley Crematorium, Coventry, alongside his wife. Sadly, with no immediate family to inherit, the entire contents and personal effects of the Bettmann residence, Elm Bank, was auctioned off on 2 and 3 April 1952.

VERNON, 1919/20 (1901–1930)

Vernon Cycle & Motor Co. Ltd, Star Yard, 30 Earl Street

Around 1901, Frank Johnstone founded the Vernon Cycle Co. at 30 Earl Street. Johnstone was born in Coventry in 1879, and from an early age worked in the Coventry cycle industry. He must have learnt his trade very quickly and skilfully as by the age of 22, he was managing his own cycle company. Why he chose the name Vernon is not known, but speculation exists that he may have purchased the business from people of the same name. This is supported by the 1901 census, showing John and Richard Vernon working in the city as 'Cycle Finishers', or, more likely, Percy Venables Vernon, who is listed as an 'Engineers Chief Draughtsman'. From its humble beginnings the company appear to have just concerned themselves with cycle production, but by around 1910, they changed their name to the Vernon Cycle & Motor Co. At this point they began to involve themselves in car and motorcycle production, but more heavily in general engineering and always maintained their production of cycles right the way through until closure in 1930.

WD, 1911–1913

Wartnaby & Draper, 21 Coundon Road, Coundon

Wartnaby & Draper were typical of the small independent manufacturers, working out of backyards in terraced housing, eager to put their previous engineering experience to use in the hope that if they proved competitive, then they could later expand and perhaps prosper. The principal men concerned were William Thomas Wade Wartnaby (1885-1925) of Market Harborough, and Alick Darby Draper (b.1884) of

A well presented 1911 WD model. They were only produced for two years. (Mortons Media)

Detail of the 1911 WD Motorcycle's vertical single-cylinder engine supplied by Monk Engineering. (Mortons Media)

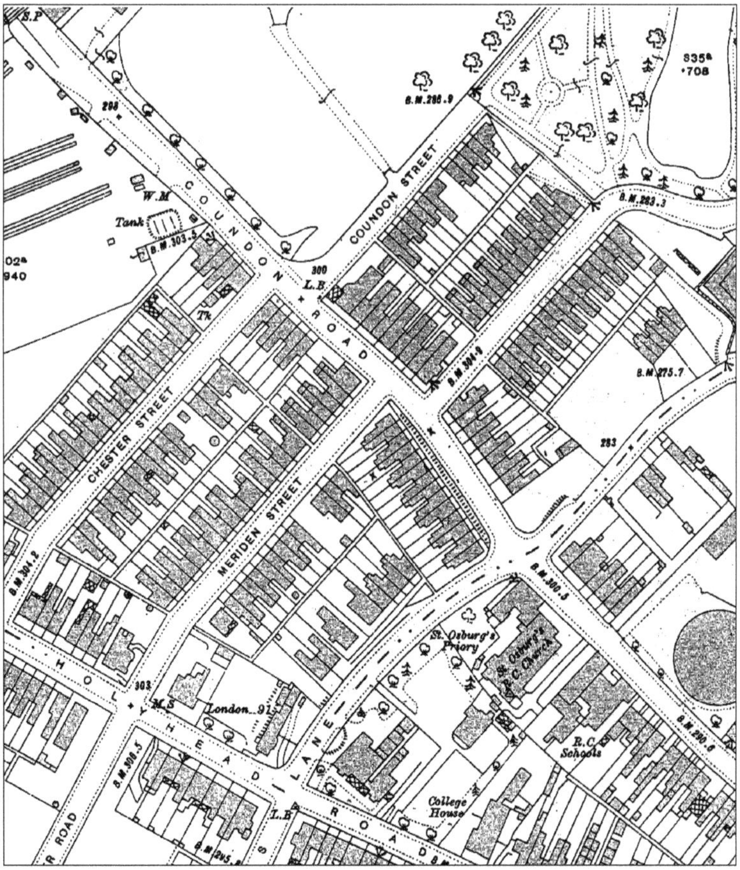

21 Coundon Road (x) – the address given for the WD motorcycle. (Ordnance Survey)

Hemel Hempstead. After studying engineering together in the Warwickshire town of Rugby, by 1911 both could be seen living at the Wartnaby family home in Market Harborough, with both being listed as 'Engineers'. Later that year, Wartnaby & Draper were known to have produced motorcycles fitted with 496cc engines built and supplied by Monk Engineering, a local firm based at 21 High Street, Coventry. It appears that W. D. sold their machines through the London based Service & Colonial Co., and also had links with the Connaught Company of Birmingham. *The Motor Cycle* of November 1911 reviewed the new W. D. machine stating: 'The W. D. motor bicycle is the joint production of two engineers named Wartnaby and Draper, who are enthusiastic motorcyclists. For some considerable time they have collaborated to design an engine for motorcycles dispensing with splash lubrication'. The only address supplied for W. D. Motors Ltd was listed as 21a Coundon Road, Coventry, but this was more likely to be a residential property with works elsewhere or to the rear. It is not certain whether Wartnaby or Draper actually lived here, yet the 1912/13 *Coventry Directory* revealed a Mr. George Needle, 'Engineer', occupying this address who may be connected. At the company's humble beginnings in 1911, there were already approximately 40 other companies competing for business in Coventry alone. Unfortunately, like so many before and like so many to follow, Wartnaby and Draper would find the motorcycle market difficult to conquer. The financial clout of larger established companies together with War looming in Europe made this virtually impossible. W. D. Motors Ltd seemingly closed after just two years and the partners went their separate ways.

(See also Service.)

An advertisment for Coventry Bicycles Ltd. Wee McGregor motorcycle. (Vintage Motor Cycle Club)

WEE McGREGOR, 1922–1925

Coventry Bicycles Ltd, Barbury & Downes, Wellington Street, Hillfields

From 1922, Coventry Bicycles Ltd of Wellington Street introduced the 'Wee McGregor' machine. This took the form of an ultra-lightweight autocycle, powered by a 170cc Hobart engine and was targeted at the cheaper end of the market. Later models incorporated a 205cc motor, and a ladies model also became available, built using a dropped open frame. In 1924, two Wee McGregor machines were entered in the Ultra-Lightweight category at the Isle of Man TT. One was ridden by D. Young, who finished in a credible 10th position. The other, ridden by F.F. Downes, failed to complete the course. The engine for the Wee McGregor was designed by a Mr Mackintosh, and it is said that around 3,500 of these machines were built by Rex-Acme. Coventry Bicycles Ltd was in fact owned by two men; a man named Barbury, and the TT entrant Downes, who were both ex-employees of the Hobart Co.

(See also Coventry B&D, Coventry B&S, Three Spires, and White Heather.)

The 1923 Wee McGregor forms part of Coventry Transport Museum's motorcycle collection. (Coventry Transport Museum)

WERNER, 1898–1901

Werner (UK) Ltd, Motor Manufacturing Co. Ltd, Motor Mills, Drapers Fields

In 1898, Harry J. Lawson's Motor Manufacturing Co. began building Werner motorcycles on one floor of the 'Motor Mills'. As with De Dion Bouton, Daimler and Bollee, Lawson had obtained the British manufacturing rights for the production of Werner machines, this time at a cost of £4,000, and was quick to put this operation into place by building some 300 machines. The Werner was first put on the market in France in 1897, but gained a bad reputation for sideslip. This was largely due to the engine being mounted above the front wheel – fitted with hot tube ignition, yet under Lawson, it was said to be, 'the first practical machine fitted with belt-drive to be sold in Britain'. By 1902, these machines were being sold by Werner Motors Ltd of 151a Regent Street, London.
(See also Lawson.)

WHEATCROFT, 1924 (1919–1924)

New Era Engineering Co., Moor Street, Earlsdon

Arthur Lynes had begun his association with the motorcycle market in 1919 with the introduction of his A.E.L. machine. The following year he began building New Era models for the Era Motor Co. of Liverpool. In 1924 he added a third marque to his name with the introduction of the Wheatcroft motorcycle offering two models for one year only. The first of these was a lightweight fitted with a 318cc Dalm engine, and the second, a larger 545cc

Blackburne-powered unit. The 'Wheatcroft' name is something of a mystery, yet may well have been connected to someone who had designed this motorcycle or developed its engine. In 1901, a Mr Harry Wheatcroft aged 43 of Cannock can be seen working in Birmingham as a mechanical engineer. By 1933, someone of the same name is seen to be residing at Union Street, Coventry, but his occupation unknown.
(See also AEL, and New Era.)

WHITE HEATHER, *c.* 1915–1925
Mackintosh, Coventry

Mackintosh was thought to have been an ex-employee of the Hobart Co., and quite possibly, Coventry Bicycles Ltd. He was said to have been the man that was also behind the 'Wee McGregor' machine, and given his Scottish name, this would seem quite plausible. Exactly who Mackintosh was though is so far unknown, but he probably moved to Coventry after the First World War to work in the motor industry, having previously worked as a motor engineer elsewhere. His 'White Heather' motorcycle is also a bit of an enigma, with no exact date for its production, limited information regarding its construction, and no address. All that is known is that Mackintosh built assembly machines using 4hp side-valve VAF engines that were built by V. Antoine Fils of Leige, Belgium. Interestingly, the 1919/20 Coventry Directory lists a 'White Heather Laundry' at Waveley Road, Spon End, but whether this has any connection is open for debate.
(See also Hobart, and Wee McGregor.)

WHITEHOUSE, 1919–1920 (1915–1922)
Whitehouse & Co. Ltd, 16 Friars Road

Walter Henry Whitehouse sold the 'Revere' motorcycle from 1915, but in 1919 also sold machines under his own name. These were quite basic 'Whitehouse' models fitted with 269cc Villiers engines, and assembled by the Sparkbrook Manufacturing Co. at Payne's Lane under contract. The 1919/20 Coventry Spennell Directory clearly lists the company as 'Whitehouse & Co. Ltd, Cycle and Motorcycle Manufacturers, Friars Road', and it appears that he continued in business as an engineer for a further two years. After 1922, all records of the company and Whitehouse seem to vanish.
(See also Revere.)

WHITE & POPPE, 1902–1922 (1899–1933)
White & Poppe Ltd, Drake Street, Lockhurst Lane & Holbrook Lane, Foleshill

White & Poppe Ltd were established in Coventry by Peter August Poppe and Alfred James White. Poppe, born in 1870, was of Norwegian origin and a highly skilled Civil Engineer. White was born in Earlsdon, Coventry also in 1870, the son of Joseph N. White, the former watch manufacturer, and Director at both the Singer and Swift cycle companies. They first met while both were visiting the Steyr small-arms factory in Austria in the early 1890s, and after a few meetings, White suggested that Poppe should move to England. After some deliberation he agreed and by September 1899 they joined forces specialising in engine making for supply. On moving to Coventry, Poppe brought with him a De Dion tricycle that he had purchased in Austria, no doubt using it to commute to work. White's family invested the majority into the new venture with White himself personally taking over the responsibility of accounts as 'General Manager of Mechanical Engineers'. Poppe, on the other hand completely took control of the design side. By 1902, the company began building their own complete motorcycles using a 5hp vertical-twin engine. Although this was to continue on a very limited scale for the next twenty years, the company concentrated their efforts more on engine supply, gaining lucrative contracts with companies such as Ariel, and later, the Morris Motor Co. The First World War was to prove instrumental in White & Poppe's future success. At the outbreak of war in 1914 the company employed some 350 workers, yet by 1918 this had reached 12,000. This was due to the large contracts being agreed by the company to build millions of munitions components, mostly made up of aluminum fuse bodies and shell-sockets. Much of this skilled work was undertaken by women who were drafted into Coventry in their thousands from all over the British Isles and beyond. They became known locally as the 'W&P Canaries' because the explosives used during their work stained their hands, face and clothing yellow. In 1920, White, the principal shareholder, sold his interest to the Dennis Co. Poppe stayed on for a further two years before joining Rover as Chief Engineer where three of his sons already worked, including Olaf Poppe as Works Manager. In 1925 Peter Poppe designed the Rover 14/45, which unfortunately proved to be a commercial disaster for the company. By 1930 Colonel Searle was drafted in to streamline departments and as a result, Poppe was sacked, and his son Olaf given six months' notice. Many thought that this was in direct connection for Poppe's earlier miscalculations, which many board members had not forgotten. The White & Poppe Co. ceased all business in 1933.

(See also P&P, and Rover.)

The White & Poppe Works based at Holbrooks. (Coventry Transport Museum)

Office staff at White & Poppe. Peter Poppe is seated in the front with Alfred White to his immediate right. (Coventry Transport Museum)

William Hubbard's Whitley Motor Co. Ltd also supplied engines. (Vintage Motor Cycle Club)

WHITLEY, 1902–1910

Whitley Motor Co. Ltd, Whitley Works, Cow Lane

The Whitley Motor Co. Ltd was yet another firm established in Coventry on the back of the fast growing motor industry. Their factory was located in Cow Lane, an ancient street crammed with timber-framed buildings. Predominately, Whitley's main purpose involved the production and supply of a range of proprietary engines, carburettors and tanks, but they also built motorcycles and forecars. These belt-driven machines were fitted with their own engines hung from the underside of the down-tube, the over-all finish of which was of a very high standard. The owner of the firm, William Hubbard, claimed that their machines 'excelled all others for strength, simplicity, bearings, material, neatness and finish'. The company appears to have closed around 1910, yet another firm, the Whitley Manufacturing Co., appear in 1919 as 'Engineers and Coachbuilders' at London Road. Whether these two companies are connected in any way is not known. Cow Lane no longer exists, being badly damaged by the bombings of the Second World War and finally being erased with the central redevelopment of the 1950s and '60s.

(See also Hubbard.)

WIGAN-BARLOW, 1921–1923

Wigan-Barlow Motors Ltd, Lowther Street, Stoke

Another small company set up in Coventry in the 1920s was that of Messrs Wigan and Barlow out of a small factory in Lowther Street. It is believed that two engineers, Aubrey John Graham-Wigan of Maidstone, and Ashworth Barlow of Scarborough founded the business. Their first registered address was a solicitor's office at 38 Bayley Lane before making the move to Lowther Street, and although it's not known where Wigan was living at this time, Barlow was seen to be residing at 35 Kingsway, Coventry. Mainly being in the business of general engineering and repair, they also developed motorcycles assembled from outsourced parts using 293cc side-valve JAP and 346cc Barr & Stroud power units. It has been reported that in 1922, consulting engineer F. Carey designed a racing motorcar for the company called the '11/40 Sports', powered by a 1795cc Meadows engine, but it is not known whether he had any involvement with their motorcycles.

WILLIAMSON, 1911–1920

A. Williamson & Co. Ltd, 77 Moor Street
Williamson Motor Co. Ltd, Cromwell Works, Cromwell Street

William and Harold Williamson had been instrumental in the early days of the Rex Motor Manufacturing Co. alongside the Pilkington brothers. But a boardroom bust-up in 1911 saw the Williamson brothers leave, Harold being appointed Sales Manager at the Singer Motor Co., and William, establishing the Williamson Motor Co. at Moor Street, a stone's throw from the Rex factory. Born in 1873 in Coventry, 'Billy', as William was known, found employment in the

Harold Williamson (left) went on to work for the Singer Co., while brother Billy Williamson set himself up in business. (Coventry Transport Museum)

city's cycle industry on leaving school, and by 1901, can be seen working as a 'Mechanic in the Cycle Trade'. Williamson's first motorcycles were 8hp flat-twin water-cooled machines, with 864cc engines supplied from the Bristol-based Douglas Co. The following year he exhibited at the International Cycle, Motorcycle and Accessories Exhibition at Olympia in London. Billy Williamson and Willy Douglas were in fact cousins, which explains why the Williamson and Douglas motorcycles of that period bear such similarities.
(See also Rex.)

WILLIS, 1907–1909
F. Willis, 333 Foleshill Road

Absolutely nothing is known about Mr F. Willis except two entries listed in the 1907 and 1909 Coventry trade directories, listing him as a 'Cycle and Motorcycle Manufacturer'. The 1901 census reveals two strong possibilities about who Mr Willis could have been – a Frank Willis of Ireland aged 24, working in Coventry as a 'Cycle Brazier', or Frank Willis of Blackpool aged 20, and working as a 'Draughtsman' in the city for a company of Mechanical Engineers. Whichever man it was, Willis, like many other men looking to succeed through motorcycle manufacture, ultimately failed and only lasted two years.

WINDRUSH, 1910–1912
Henry Preece, 44 Gordon Street

Henry Preece learned his trade as a cycle maker, before applying his engineering skills to building his own motorcycle from 1910, out of the backyard of his terrace house in Gordon Street. The 'Windrush', as it was called, was said to have been named after the river which runs through the Gloucestershire village of Bourton-on-the-Water, where his wife hailed from. The motorcycle was available with a 500cc JAP engine but on a very limited scale, only made to order. Unfortunately, not many were ordered, and this marque was only produced for two years. Although Preece was still seen to be living at Gordon Street in 1921, nothing is known of his business activities after 1912.

YORK, 1927–1930
York-Motorfahrzeugefabrik (Robert Sturm), Austria & Germany
W.J. Green, Omega Works, Croft Road

This marque was built by W.J. Green of the Omega Works in Coventry to a design supplied by Austrian, Robert Sturm. Sturm then sold these machines under the 'York' name, out of his York-Motorfahrzeugefabrik – his factories in Austria and Germany. This arrangement lasted for some three years, with models available in various sized JAP engines. Green was a former employee of the Premier Co. in Coventry before the First World War, where his job was to drum up business in Europe and beyond. It would be likely that he first came into contact with Robert Sturm during these years.
(See also Omega.)

APPENDIX 1

MOTORCYCLE MANUFACTURERS WITH CLOSE LINKS TO COVENTRY

The following list of motorcycle manufacturers may well have had connections with Coventry, and in many cases sourced parts from the city, but their location places them just outside the comprehensive list. Even so, any further information about these companies, their products and the individuals concerned would be greatly received by Coventry Transport Museum.

ARDEN, 1912–1922

Arden Motor Co. Ltd, Kenilworth Road, Balsall Common & Blacksmith Corner, Berkswell

The Arden Motor Co. Ltd was established in rural Berkswell in 1912. It was said to have been started by a local builder named Mr Isherwood with a nominal capital of £1,500. This was divided equally between himself and an engineer and building contractor from Coventry, and another engineer from Kidderminster, the names of which are sadly unknown. Arden as a company were primarily concerned with building cycle cars, light cars and general engineering, but soon developed complete motorcycles of their own on a limited scale of 269cc two-stroke Villiers motors. The Arden name derives from the ancient Forest of Arden which once covered the Warwickshire region.

COVENTRY ACE, 1924

Coventry Ace, Queens Road, Kenilworth

This rare model was offered in March 1924 as an open-frame luxurious miniature machine, aimed at the growing female market. Powered by a 147cc Villiers engine, it was designed and built by Mr Alfred. E. Shakeshaft at small works in Queens Road, Kenilworth. Prior to the introduction of the 'Coventry Ace', Coventry-born Shakeshaft worked in Leamington Spa for his father's insurance agency as a 'Commercial Clerk'.

CREST, 1923–1924

The Crest Motor Co., Blackdown Mills, Leamington Spa

The Crest Motor Co. built motorcycles fitted with 349cc Barr & Stroud sleeve-valve engines. They were based at 'Blackdown Mills' in Royal Leamington Spa, but nothing is known about the men who founded the firm. It is probable that these machines were simply assembled using parts sources from local suppliers.

GEORGE ELIOT, 1902–1905 (1890–1910)

Birch & Co., Market Place & Princess Street, Nuneaton.

The company of Birch & Co. began at the Foleshill Cycle Works at Windmill Lane, Coventry in 1890 as cycle makers, before moving to Priory

John North Birch stands with his George Eliot motor-bicycle. (Coventry Transport Museum)

Mills, Coventry the following year. John North Birch* later separated himself from the family business, setting himself up at Nuneaton to make the 'George Eliot' motorcycle by 1902. It was a primitive model, not unusual for the period, but of a high-quality finish and exhibited at the Stanley Show that year. In 1903, he sold the designs to this machine to the Bradbury Co. of Oldham. Although often assumed, the motorcycle was not only named after the famous novelist, but also after John's father who was called George Eliot Birch. In 1905, John North Birch emigrated to New Zealand to apparently find his fortune, and surprisingly, left his wife and three children behind. In New Zealand he established the Marlborough and Carlton car companies, yet never returned home to England, and died at the age of 78 in 1945 in Gisborne.

*John North Birch is not connected to the Perks & Birch 'Motor Wheel' of 1899–1901; this was invented by Edwin Perks and Frank Birch of Coventry.

MARLOW, 1920–1922

Marlow Motorcycles Ltd,
20a Emscote Road, Warwick

Marlow were a small company that built machines powered by two-stroke 269cc Villiers and 292cc JAP sv engines for two years only. They were located at Warwick but most probably sourced most of the remaining parts needed from Birmingham and Coventry. Two decades before, a 17-year-old Edwin Spencer Marlow can be seen working in Coventry as an 'Engineers Apprentice' in the 1901 census, and he may well be connected.

PRIORY, 1919–1926

Priory Engine Co.,
82 Priory Road, Kenilworth

The Priory Engine Co. was based at Kenilworth, near Coventry. They took their name from their address, situated near to where St Mary's Abbey once stood. The firm made motorcycles fitted with Arden engines, plus 147cc and 269cc single-cylinder Villiers units. When production ceased around 1926, the remaining spares were said to have been discovered some years later at Holland's, the Motorcycle Dealers, at Hearsall Lane, Coventry.

SHIRLEY, 1912

W.J. Shirley, Coventry Road, Meriden & Hampton-in-Arden

Page 10 of *The Coventry Graphic* of September 1912 shows an advertisment for a Mr W.J. Shirley, 'Cycle & Motor Cycle Builder and Repairer'. It claims that he was the maker of the famous 'Berkswell' cycle. If this is the case then perhaps his motorcycle went by this name also. The 1901 census shows a number of men with the surname of Shirley working in the cycle industry in Coventry and Warwickshire of whom may be related.

APPENDIX 2

MOTORCYCLE MYSTERIES

The following is a list of manufacturers and marques that may have been associated with Coventry. If anyone has any further information, then please contact the author at Coventry Transport Museum so that we can amend and update our records accordingly.

ARGYLL, 1913

Argyll Ltd, Argyll Street, Stoke

It has been suggested that this marque originated from the Stoke area of Coventry. Studying the local map reveals an Argyll Street in Stoke, Coventry which would surely indicate the address of this small company. The *Old Motorcycle* of September 1986 has a picture of an 'Argyll-JAP' belonging to a gentleman in Scotland, yet the author states that it was built in Stoke, Coventry. Whether this Argyll has any links with the Scottish car manufacturers is unlikely. Incidentally, the 1919/20 Coventry Spennell Directory shows John William Wartnaby (of Wartnaby & Draper) to be living at 38 Argyll Street, Stoke. Considering that W.D. motorcycles were made from 1911–1913 then Wartnaby may well be the man behind Argyll Ltd

(See also W.D.)

ARIEL, 1906–1925 (1898–1965)

Ariel, Cheylesmore Works and Quinton Works, Parkside

Known to have been a Birmingham manufacturer of motorcycles from 1898–1965, Ariel had early links with Coventry and were known to have had cars built there. These were manufactured at the Ordnance Works from 1906 to 1925, but stopped in between, during the First World War. Ariel used Coventry-built White & Poppe engines early on, and were also linked to the Swift Cycle Co. through Lord Randolph Churchill and Harvey Du Cros. James Starley and William Hillman first used the 'Ariel' name in 1871 for a design of an 'Ordinary' bicycle in Coventry, but whether any motorcycles of the same name were ever developed here is not clear.

(See also Swift.)

BOLLEE, 1896–1898

Bollee, H.J. Lawson, Lower Ford Street, & Motor Mills, Drapers Field

In 1896, Lawson paid Frenchman Leon Bollee £20,000 for the British manufacturing and patent rights to build Bollee machines. The task was given to the Humber Co. who produced the first Bollee voiturette as 'three-wheel motor carriages', but whether they were actually marketed and sold under the Bollee name from Coventry is not known. However, after a fire at the Humber factory, Lawson formed the Coventry Motor Co., and all future Bollee machines were sold as 'Coventry Motettes'.

(See also Lawson.)

BRENDA, 1905–1921 (1905–1924)

Brenda Cycle & Motor Co. Ltd, 64 Moor Street, Earlsdon

Nothing at all is known about this company except that they were featured in an early 1905 Coventry Directory and again on an independently researched list of Earsldon manufacturers from 1921–1924. From the name, the Brenda Cycle & Motor Co., it would appear obvious that they were a manufacturer of cycles, yet if they were also concerned with motor engines, then it would seem logical to somehow put the two together. Why the name Brenda was chosen is also a complete mystery.

BRITANNIA, 1929

Britannia Cycle & Motor Co., 52 Cox Street

As the name of this company would suggest, Britannia concerned themselves with cycles and motor vehicles, yet whether this was in production or sales and repair is unknown. No buildings of this date survive on Cox Street, the area being redeveloped for the building of Coventry University.

BRITISH CYCLE, 1933–1934

British Cycle & Motor Cycle Ltd, Warwick Road

This company was listed in the 1933/34 Coventry Directory under 'Cycle Manufacturers', but again their title indicates the production of motorcycles as well.

BRITON, 1897–1898

Briton Cycle Co. Ltd, Oddfellows Hall, Little Park Street

The Briton Cycle Co. Ltd were seen listed in the Applications for Registration of Trade Marks for 1897 as 'Cycle Manufacturers', yet their other business activities also stated, 'makers of bicycles, tricycles, motor-bicycles, motor tricycles, auto cars and horseless carriages'.

BROUGH, 1918

George Brough and Percy Mayo, Coventry Eagle

An article in the *Vintage Motorcycle Magazine* of August 2005 states that George Brough served in France (1914–1918) with Percy Mayo of the Coventry Eagle Co. After the war, the author states that they both worked on the first Brough Superior together, and that Mayo was 'almost certainly behind the distinctive shape of the tank'. The nephew of Percy Mayo, Douglas Mayo, also gives his uncle credit for the majority of work on this motorcycle. Other links include Coventry Eagle motorcycles of this period, particularly the 'Flying 8' sharing a similar design of tank, and the first Brough Superior frames being supplied by the Montgomery Co. of Coventry. In further support of this, the press cuttings of Muriel Hind housed at Coventry Transport Museum reveal that George Brough rented a cottage near her and husband Dick Lord (of the Coventry Motor Mart) at Corley, Warwickshire during the war years, and on occasion borrowed motorcycles from them for trips out into the country.
(See also Coventry Eagle.)

BUCKINGHAM, 1914–1928

J.F. Buckingham, Buckingham Engine Works, Spon Street, & 15 Dover Street/ Holyhead Road

James Frank Buckingham was a known car maker in Coventry, yet whether he also extended to building a motorcycle is debatable. In 1912 he helped form the company of Manley & Buckingham at Spon Street, but by December of that year, Manley had severed all ties. Under the new title of J.F. Buckingham, he developed the 'Chota' cyclecar, which was fitted with his own 6hp 746cc single-cylinder engine. The next year Buckingham raced this machine in the Cyclecar Handicap at Brookland's, finishing in third position. During the 1920s he was listed locally under 'Engineer and Motor Manufacturer' at Dover Street. During the First World War, Buckingham also found brief fame as the inventor of the incendiary bullet that was later used for anti-Zeppelin work, and 'Give 'em a burst of Buckingham's' became a well-used phrase at that time. Some 26,000,000 of these were said to have been produced at Dover Street, earning Buckingham an OBE.

CENTURY, 1902–1905

Century Ltd, Motor Mills, Drapers Fields

The Century Engineering & Motor Co. were actually a London-based firm at Willesden Junction, but speculation exists which suggests that some models were assembled under agreement through H.J. Lawson at the Coventry 'Motor Mills' off Sandy Lane. Considering that some Century machines were built using MMC engines of Lawson's Coventry-based Motor Manufacturing Co., then

there may be some substance in this. Australian-born Selwyn Francis Edge (1868–1940) was also said to have been connected with the company. On viewing the 1894/5 *Cyclist Year Book*, it confirms that in 1894, Edge is living in Upper Norwood, London, but the following year, at 26 Hill Street, Coventry. At this time he was licensed as a 'cycle racer', but later went on to become famous for racing cars and even motorboats in trials and competitions. More famously, he also went on to become Managing Director of the Napier Motor Co. in London.
(See also Lawson, and MMC.)

COVENTRY DUPLEX, 1907
Coventry Duplex, address unknown

This machine can be seen advertised in the 4 December 1907 edition of *The Motor Cycle*. Apart from the fact that it was powered by a Motosacoche attachment, little more is known about this motorised bicycle. Using the name of 'Coventry' in its title, should, one would suspect, indicate that it was built in the very city of the same name.

COVENTRY EMBLEM, 1920
Coventry Emblem, address unknown

The Coventry Emblem was thought to have been developed in Coventry in 1920. The machine was said to have been powered by a two-stroke 296cc Villiers engine fitted to a basic frame. Coventry Emblem may well have been connected to the Coventry Ensign Co. who ran the following year, but this is only speculation. Many Coventry motorcycle companies incorporated 'Coventry' into the names of their products. This stems back to many of the early cycle manufacturers which earned such a good reputation in design and craftsmanship that having the Coventry 'stamp' was a seen as a sign of quality and engineering excellence, and respected throughout the world.

CRESCENT, 1911–1915
Rudge-Whitworth Ltd, Crow Lane

This marque has been suggested as being built by Rudge-Whitworth as an economical and practical model. The 'Crescent' name was seen to be registered by the company in August 1911. It was powered by a 269cc Villiers two-stroke engine with separate magneto for its ignition, was belt-driven, and of very basic design. Why it was given the name of 'Crescent' is puzzling, but given the date was probably built in large quantities for the War Service. However, there is a Crescent Motors Ltd running from 1911–1915 at Walsall and Birmingham listed in the *Beaulieu Encyclopaedia of the Automobile* Volume 1 by Nick Georgano that may well be related.
(See also Rudge.)

DE HAVILLAND, 1911–1913
De Havilland, Warwick Row

The De Havilland name became famous in the aviation world from the First World War and subsequently produced renowned and celebrated aeroplanes such as the Tiger Moth and Mosquito. The man concerned was Geoffrey De Havilland, yet whether he was actually the man attributed to developing a motorcycle in Coventry, or one of his brothers, is open for debate. He was born in 1882 at Hazlemere in Buckinghamshire, yet his family moved to Nuneaton, Warwickshire in the 1890s. Geoffrey and his older brother Ivan studied engineering there, and it is said that they built an early motorcycle before passing on the designs to their younger brother, Hereward. Later improvements were supposedly sold to Alick and Cecil Burney who went on to form the Blackburne Engine Co. Geoffrey's older brother Ivon was also said to have worked for the Daimler Motor Co. at Coventry, but died in 1905. Considering all this, if a De Havilland motorcycle was being marketed from 1911 at Warwick Row, Coventry, then it has to be either Geoffrey or Hereward De Havilland who was responsible.

DREADNOUGHT, 1902
H. Karslake, address unknown

This name features on an old Coventry Transport Museum list but supplies no dates, address or any other information. Two companies supposedly used the Dreadnought name, one in Birmingham from 1915–1922 by W.A. Lloyd, and the second from 1902 by Harold 'Oily' Karslake. He was said to have built this machine using a De Dion Bouton engine, so perhaps the link may once again be with H.J. Lawson and the 'Motor Mills' in Coventry. Karslake later went on to work for William Brough as an engineer.
(See also Lawson.)

HERNER, 1923

Herner Engineering Co., address unknown

A motorcycle of this name was said to have been built in Coventry in 1923 by the Herner Engineering Co. The machine was fitted with a 147cc engine, probably Villiers, and had an oversized windshield to protect the rider from the elements. Who Herner was or where he was situated in Coventry is unknown. The 1901 census shows ten males that share the Herner name but none local to Coventry and none connected to the cycle, motor or engineering industries. One named Henry J. Herner, aged 14 of Edmonton, Middlesex is listed without an occupation but would appear to be the best bet.

JONES, 1904

E. Jones, Byron Street, Hillfields

In addition to the two known Coventry Jones motorcycles, there may well have been a third. A British motorcycle directory of 2003 lists a Jones motorcycle of 1904. It does not mention an address for Mr Jones but does state that it was fitted with a Coronet engine. Coronet was a Coventry company who made motorcycles from 1903 to 1906 and were known to also supply engines. An early Coventry directory of 1894 reveals a Mr E. Jones as a 'Bicycle Manufacturer' at Byron Street, situated in the Hillfields area of the city, so perhaps by 1904 he had progressed to build a motorcycle.

MOHAWK, 1912–1925

Mohawk Cycle Co., 201 Foleshill Road

This company was actually a well-established cycle firm established by Thomson and James and based at 39 Chalk Farm in London. They began producing motorcycles from 1903–1925, but there have been suggestions that the machines themselves were actually built in Coventry. In August 1911, a James Williams of 2 Alexandra Road, Hornsey in London registered the 'Mohawk' name, and his occupation listed as 'Cycle Manufacturer & Dealer of Bicycles Ordinary or Motor'. By 1912, there is indeed a Mohawk Cycle Co. seen to be based at 201 Foleshill Road, so perhaps James Williams was connected with this arrangement.

(See also Young.)

NEW ENGLAND, 1924

The New England Cycle Co., Radford Road

As seen in the 1924 *Coventry Directory* under 'Cycle Manufacturers' at Radford Road, but with an advert on p. 691 stating 'cycle and motor cycle manufacturers.

NEW IMPERIAL, 1940 (1912–1940)

New Imperial Motors Ltd, Dale Street

The New Imperial motorcycle was introduced in 1912 at Loveday Street in Birmingham by Norman Duckwood Downs (b. 1875), a former Cycle Manufacturer. When Downs died in 1936, the company began to fall into financial difficulty, and by 1940, the manufacturing rights were bought by Jack Sangster, at that point the Triumph Chief. Production of the New Imperial was then said to have been moved to Triumph's Dale Street factory. These works were then almost completely destroyed the same year during the Blitz, but it has been reported that a few New Imperials actually rolled off the production line.

(See also Triumph.)

NOMAD-EARLY, 1920s

W.R. Early, address unknown

The 'Nomad-Early' is featured in an A–Z of British motorcycle manufacturers, suggesting the machine to have been developed in Coventry. It is believed that this took the form of a small two-stroke that had an exhaust pipe coming out from the side of the cylinder. Nomad was the name of the motorcycle, and Early is either the builder, make of engine used, or both. The 1901 census does reveal a William R. Early, aged 14 of London, and working as an 'Apprentice Engine Fitter', so perhaps this is the man responsible, moving to Coventry later.

RANGER, 1913 (1901–1915)

Ranger Cycle Car Co. Ltd, West Orchard

E.J. West of the Ranger Cycle Car Co. built motorcycles under the Progress name from 1901–1908. From 1913, and at an address at West Orchard he designed and marketed a cycle car known as the 'Ranger', but it is not known for certain if this was also transferred to a motorcycle

of the same name. These Ranger's were powered by 946cc 8hp V-Twin Precision engines of chain-drive until 1914.
(See also Progress.)

REX-REMO, 1902–1914

Rex Motor Manufacturing Co., Earlsdon Works, Osborne Road

The Rex Co. experimented with a wealth of concepts and motors in the production of their early vehicles, the results of which gained some unusual names including Rexette, Ast-Rex, Airex and Rex-Simplex. The Rex-Remo was another name used, but it's unclear whether this was the name of a motorcar, motorcycle, or both.
(See also Rex.)

ROYAL-RYDAL, 1903–1904

Royal-Rydal, address unknown

Another early marque thought to be developed in Coventry, yet nothing conclusive shows up for the Rydal name in the 1901 census. In fact only one man in the country holds this name, and four women, one of which is Warwickshire-based. For various reasons though, not everyone was census listed in 1901, including Harry J. Lawson, who may well have had some involvement here. Alternatively, Rydal of course may well have been a foreign subject arriving after 1901. Nevertheless, the company was said to have made cycles before later developing a motor-bicycle powered by a clip-on Minerva engine, but nothing more is known.
(See also Lawson.)

SPRINGWELL, 1920

E.J. Norton, address unknown

It has been publicised that the 'Springwell' was a prototype design based on a unique pivoted-fork suspension system consisting of leaf-springs.
It was built by E.J. Norton who ran a wielding and engineering company in Coventry. These patented designs were said to have been offered to larger companies but nothing materialised. Whether this Mr Norton is a relation of the Norton Cycle & Motor Co. of 1905 is not known, and neither is the address he operated from.
(See also Norton.)

SUDBROOK, 1919–1920

Sudbrook, address unknown

Another motorcycle listed in an A–Z of British motorcycle manufacturers to originate from Coventry but with no address supplied. From 1919, it was said to be powered by a 269cc Villiers engine using proprietary parts for no more than one year only, but no further information given. As a surname, only five males show up in the 1901 census, but none local to Coventry and none associated with the cycle or engineering trades. The youngest is Thomas Sudbrook aged 12 of

Humber works rider Len Crisp (right), winner of countless trials during the 1920s and '30s. (Coventry Transport Museum)

Leyton, London, which would place him at the age of 30 or 31 in 1919/20, provided he was the man responsible.

TOOTH, 1914 (1914–1920)

J.N. Tooth, Humber Road, Stoke

This 50cc lightweight motorcycle was said to have been built at Humber Road from August 1914 by a Mr Tooth. The engine was said to have been attached above the rear wheel, belt-driven, with the rest of the machine generally made up from other outsourced parts. The 1901 census reveals a Mr Charles T. Tooth aged 27 from Manchester, now living in Coventry and working as an 'Iron Turner in a Cycle Shop'. However the 1919/20 Coventry Spennell Directory lists a J.N. Tooth under 'Engineers' at 155 St George Road, which happens to be a stone's throw from Humber Road. The residential section of the same directory lists him as James Newman Tooth living at 37 Folly Lane in Coventry, again off Humber Road. The 1901 census shows a James N. Tooth aged 35 of Manchester now working in Gateshead as a 'Fitter Toolmaker', so it would seem likely that he later moved to Coventry and is the older brother of Charles.

WILSON-KNEE, 1923

Wilson-Knee Ltd, address unknown

In the October 1990 edition of *Classic Motorcycle*, a Suffolk gentleman wrote to one of the magazine reporters, stating that he had reference to a 1923 Wilson-Knee four-cylinder motorcycle seen in the *Model Engineer* magazine for May 1956, and wished to know more about it. The reporter replied by saying he had no knowledge about an actual motorcycle of that kind, but did say that he had found reference in *The Motor Cycle* of May 1923 of an article and photographs of the Wilson-Knee four-cylinder 'swash plate engine', built by 'two Coventry engineers', the report saying, 'The experimental engine has given particularly smooth running'. The 1901 census shows some 268 men with the surname of Knee, although none bear any relevance to Coventry. Fred Knee aged 27 of Swindon working as an 'Engine Fitter' seems the most promising entry.

YOUNG, 1919–21

Mohawk Motor & Cycle Co. Ltd, 201 Foleshill Road

This machine was simply made up of a 'clip-on' engine fitted to the rear wheel of a standard bicycle for easy use. Initially, 269cc Mohawk two-stroke engines were used, before the firm opted for 131cc motors made by the Waltham Engineering Co. based in North London. This idea was hardly enterprising at this time and the Young motorised bicycle lasted less than two years from 1919 until 1921.
(See also Mohawk.)

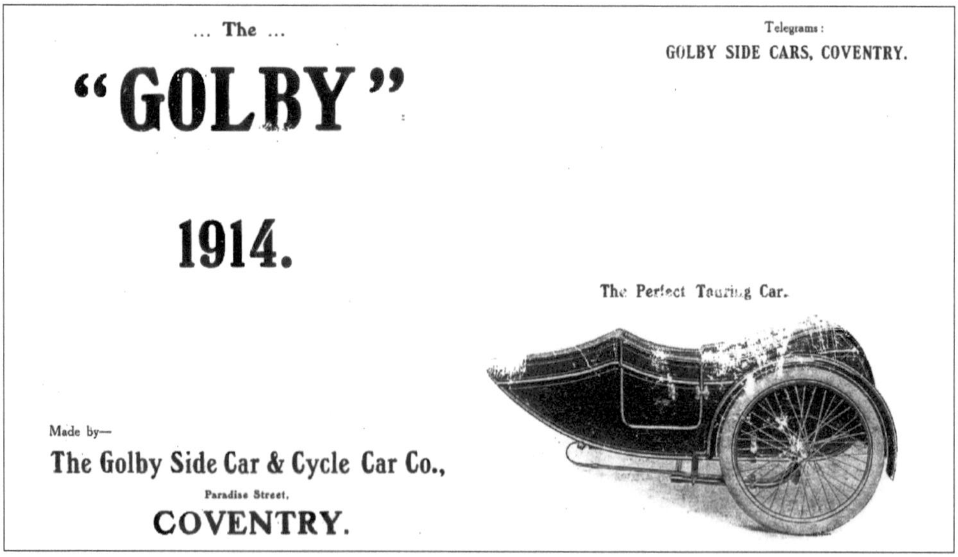

The Golby Co. supplied sidecars to the War Office in 1914. (Coventry Transport Museum)

APPENDIX 3

COVENTRY SIDECAR MANUFACTURERS

Name	*Address*	*Dates of manufacture*
Acme	Lincoln Street	1911–1922
Broadway	King William Street	1913
Brenda	Moor Street	1921–1924
Coventry Eagle	Stoney Stanton Road	1913–1924
Coventry Victor	Cox Street	1919–1938
Cross & Ellis	Clay Lane	1919
Gloria	Much Park Street	1908–1920
Golby	Paradise Street	1914
Godiva	Spon Street	1913
Grindlay	Shakleton Road	1920–1934
Hazelwood	West Orchard	1905–1923
Humber	Lower Ford Street	1913–1920
Lea-Francis	Lower ford Street	1912–1924
Mills-Fulford	Stoney Stanton Road	1901–1937
Monopole	Foleshill Road	1920–1924
Montgomery	Lower Ford Street	1905–1930
Omega	Croft Road	1920
Premier	Read Street	1910–1914
Regent	Gosford Street	1919–1920
Rex	Osborne Road	1912–1924
Rover	Rover Road	1911–1921
Rudge-Whitworth	Crow Lane	1912–1933
Sherbourne	Holyhead Road	1913
Sparkbrook	Payne's Lane	1922
Smith	Foleshill Road	1933–1934
Swallow	Holbrook Lane	1928–1946
Triumph	Priory Street	1925–1936
Whitley	London Road	1922–1929
Williamson	Moor Street	1920

A finely crafted Mills-Fulford two-seater sidecar. (Coventry Transport Museum)

Triumph built their own sidecars as well as cycles, motorcycles and cars. (Coventry Transport Museum)

APPENDIX 4

TIMELINE OF COVENTRY MOTORCYCLE INDUSTRY EVENTS, 1895–2008

1895 A German-built Hildebrand-Wolfmuller machine is tested at the Butts Cycle Track, Coventry by Triumph Manager and co-founder, Mauritz J. Schulte. American Edward Joel Pennington begins developing motorcycles to his designs at Harry J. Lawson's newly acquired 'Motor Mills'. Walter Payne creates a petrol engine in Coventry.

1896 A French-made Wolfmuller & Geisenhof motorcycle is tested by Harry J. Lawson around the city. Cycle makers Bayliss, Thomas & Co. begin making the Excelsior machine at Lower Ford Street, reputedly Britain's first production motorcycle. Humber develops their first motorcycle, while the Accles motor-tricycle is also made. A Coventry-built Beeston 1½hp tricycle takes part in the first London to Brighton run.

1897 The Coventry Motette and MMC machines are developed through Lawson at Parkside and Conduit Yard, both based on the De Dion Bouton principle. Enoch J. West builds his first 'Progress' experimental machines at Foleshill.

1898 Coventry Eagle build their first motorcycle, while Rover begins experimenting with motorised designs. Frederick W. Allard of Allard & Co. builds his first motorcycle at his

Coventry Eagle became one of the longest-running motorcycle manufacturers in the city. (Coventry Transport Museum)

A Pennington four-seater forecar stands alone on a floor at Lawson's 'Motor Mills'. (Coventry Transport Museum)

The Singer Motor-Wheel draws a crowd outside the Canterbury Street Works with Edwin Perks driving, Frank Birch back right and Herbert Duret nearside. (Coventry Transport Museum)

Moor Street Works in Earlsdon. A Pennington-Sturmey machine is built. A British Werner is made under licence by Lawson while the Swift Co. builds their first motorcycle.

1899 Perks & Birch invent the Motor-Wheel at their 'Rockland' Works, Foleshill. Bicycle manufacturers Riley begin experimenting with motorcycles. In July, Humber works rider Bert Yates wins the first motorcycle race to be staged in Britain at the Butts Cycle Track on a Humber machine.

1900 Singer makes their first motorcycle using the Perks & Birch Motor-Wheel. Payne & Bates unveil their 'Godiva' machine. Lawson offers a motorcycle under his own name, while E.J. Pennington returns home to America under a cloud of controversy.

1901 The turn of the century sees Coventry's involvement with the motorcycle increase. New firms involved include Centaur, Clarendon, Clarke, Cluley & Co., Gorton, Hamilton, Hobart, and Townend. The Rex Motor Manufacturing Co. relocates from Birmingham to Coventry, taking over Allard in Earlsdon. Meanwhile a Phelon-Humber is tested by the Humber Co., and F.J. Osborn develops a motorcycle in the city.

1902 Coventry cycle makers Triumph produce their first motorcycle at their Dale Street factory. The Acme Motor Co. also develops a machine at Earlsdon, and Charles Bourquin builds his 'Aurora' at Norfolk Street. Other new manufacturers include Dalton & Wade, Davison, Hillman, Stanley, White & Poppe, and Whitley. The Rex Co. also builds the 'Mountaineer' motorcycle under contract.

1903 Smith & Molesworth begin the manufacture of their 'Alert' motorcycle at Freeth Street, followed by machines introduced by Coronet, Coventry Challenge, Mills-Fulford, H.W. Clarke and Starley. Muriel Hind becomes possibly the first British woman to own and ride a motorcycle.

1904 The Dux Motor Manufacturing Co. builds a motorcycle at their Earlsdon factory. William Hubbard and the Lancer Motor Co. also begin production. H.J. Lawson is imprisoned after being found guilty of conspiracy to defraud.

1905 The Automobile Association is founded. The Calcott Brothers manufacture their first motorcycle at Much Park Street, as do the Norton Cycle & Motor Co. at Binley Road.

1906 Coventry-based Riley cease production of motorcycles and concentrate on cars, while Arno begins at their factory at Gosford Street. Lawson's Motor Safety Co. market a ladies motorcycle, but this is shortlived.

1907 Johnson, Hurley & Martin begin the production of the 'Alpha' motorcycle at Gosford Street. The Condor Motor Co. releases a motorcycle to add to their car output. Cromwell develops a machine at Queen Street while F. Willis follows suit at Foleshill Road. Birmingham company Quadrant relocate to Earlsdon after liquidation. The first Isle of Man TT Race held

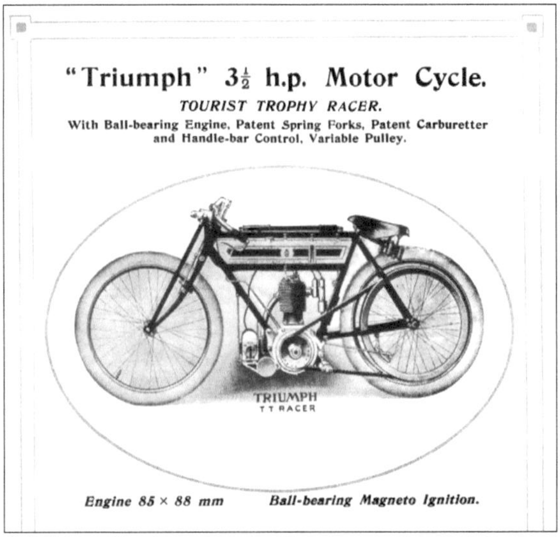

The Triumph TT model of 1908. (Coventry Transport Museum)

Rex workers take a break from building forecars at the Osborne Road Works. (Coventry Transport Museum)

with seventeen riders registering. One includes Robert Ayton on his Coventry-built Ayton-Riley machine, and another, a Rex ridden by W.M. Heaton, takes a bronze medal.

1908 William Hillman's Premier Cycle Co. manufactures their first motorcycle at Read Street. J. Marshall wins the Isle of Man TT Senior class race on a Triumph. The first Brooklands race is held with Gordon McMinnies the winner on his 3.5hp TT Triumph known as 'Puffing Billy'.

1909 The Isle of Man TT brings little joy for Coventry manufactures Rex and Triumph, with nine Rex and six Triumph machines failing to complete the course. The best positions obtained by each were O.C. Godfrey's 4th place on a Rex, and W.F. Newsome's 3rd place on a Triumph.

1910 The Cycle & Motor Cycle Manufacturers and Traders Union, forerunner of the current Motor Cycle Industry Association, is founded in Coventry. Cycle makers Rudge begin making motorcycles at Crow Lane. Humber takes over the Centaur Co. The Harris Cycle Co. releases their shortlived 'Coventry' machine. Dingley Bros Ltd venture into motorcycle production while Henry Preece builds his 'Windrush' model.

1911 Hazlewood begin making motorcycles at their West Orchard Works, and Montgomery moves their production from Bury St Edmonds to Coventry. Other new manufacturers include Alfred Noble, Gilbert Jones, Lea Francis, Maxim, Mead, Meri, Monopole, Roulette, Wartnaby & Draper, and Williamson, based at Moor Street. Meanwhile, Clarendon stop the production of motorcycles and Quadrant move production back to Birmingham. P.J. Evans finishes 1st in the Isle of Man TT junior division on a Humber. E.J. Pennington dies in America aged 53.

1912 A. Barnett releases his 'Invicta' machine, and Sparkbrook start making motorcycles at their Payne's Lane factory. At Berkswell, the Arden Motor Co. is founded. Smith & Molesworth cease production of motorcycles. Rudge and Singer gain the top three positions at the 500cc Singer Cup Scratch Race at Brookland's. Muriel Hind marries Dick Lord of the Rex Co.

1913 Triumph Managing Director Siegfried Bettmann becomes Mayor of Coventry, the first non-British subject ever to do so. ARC begin making a motorcycle at Lincoln Street, while Atlas does the same at Hill Street. Rover wins the Senior Manufacturers' Team Award at the Isle of Man TT.

1914 AEC begin making machines at Stoney Stanton Road. The Premier Cycle Co. offers the 'Coventry Premier' machine. The Arno Motor Co. market a 'Red Arno' model. Siegfried Bettmann is forced to resign as Mayor in a wave of anti-German hysteria after the outbreak of war. Rudge's Cyril Pullin gains a victory in the Senior Isle of Man TT.

1915 W.H. Whitehouse promotes the 'Revere' machine at Friars Road. The Singer and Swift companies both decide to cease production of motorcycles and instead concentrate on cars. The Calcott Brothers follow suit, while the Centaur name is dropped by Humber.

1916 The annual number of new motorcycles registered for road use reaches 150,000 in Britain. The Premier Cycle Co. ends the production of the 'Mead' motorcycle. Much general manufacturing in Coventry and the rest of Britain suffers.

1917 After supplying some 30,000 Type 'H' machines for military service, Triumph motorcycles earn the nickname 'Trusty Triumphs', such was their reliability.

1918 The First World War comes to an end. Many Coventry companies count the cost of both suffering sales, and lives lost to fellow workers.

1919 The conclusion of war ignites a host of new motorcycle marques created in the city, including AEL, CMM, Coventry Challenge, Coventry Ensign, Coventry Star, Coventry Victor, Kenilworth, Omega, Remington, Stafford, Stan, Vernon, and Whitehouse. The majority of these companies were to be very shortlived.

1920 Gordon Francis and Arthur Barnett join forces and establish Francis-Barnett at Lower Ford Street. Meanwhile, Bayliss, Thomas & Co. moves their Excelsior motorcycle production out of the same works to Tyseley, Birmingham. The Coventry Acme Co. is established. The Coventry Regent, Kingsway, Marseal and New Era motorcycles are introduced.

1921 The Rex Co. merges with Acme to form Rex-Acme. GSD motorcycles are offered by Mr R. Grant at Smithford Street, and George McKenzie begins manufacturing autocycles in the city. William Green markets a machine called the 'Omegette', and Wigan-Barlow begin production at Lowther Street. Singer concentrates future production on cars. William Hillman, the founder of the Premier and Sparkbrook Companies, dies at his Keresley home. Siegfried Bettmann unveils a memorial at London Road cemetery to sixty-six Triumph workers who lost their lives in the First World War.

A Swift motorcycle of 1913, two years before all motorcycle production stopped in order to concentrate on cars. (Coventry Transport Museum)

A 1921 Francis-Barnett with a two-stroke 2.5hp Villiers engine. (Coventry Transport Museum)

George Ravenhall on a Rover at Coventry Road, Ryton-on-Dunsmore. (Ron Ravenhall)

Stanley Glanfield in 1928 about to embark on his global tour. (Kate Button)

1922 The Caesar Cycle Co. produces their first motorcycle at Hertford Street. Other new manufacturers include Coventry Mascot, McKechnie, Packman & Poppe, Ravenhall & Hailstone, and Wee McGregor. The Sparkbrook Co. begin selling their 'Spark' machine. Rex merges with neighbours Acme to form Rex-Acme. White & Poppe cease all production.

1923 Specialist engineers Grindlay-Peerless begin building competition machines in Spon End. Coventry Bicycles Ltd release their Coventry B&D and B&S models. Others include Cameron Croft, Dart, Mars, and Morton-Adam, based at Foleshill Road. Saxelby's Ltd begins selling motorcycles under the 'Saxel' and 'Saxessories' marques. Hobart merges with Acme. Motorcycle racing pioneer Bert Yates dies aged 54.

1924 Johnson & Tyler build a motorcycle at Chapel Street. W. Jones does the same at Clarendon Street. Wheatcroft develops a machine at Moor Street through the New Era Co.

1925 Morton-Adam stop production of their motorcycle after just two years to concentrate on general engineering. Harry J. Lawson, one of the founders of the British motor industry, dies aged 73. Gilmour Packmann of Packman & Poppe is killed under suspicious circumstances at their Moor Street factory. W.L. Handley wins the Isle of Man TT junior race on a Rex-Acme.

1926 The Midland Motor Cylinder Co. develops a motorcycle at Trafalgar Street. The Sparkbrook Co. falls into difficulty and closes. W. L. Handley finishes 2nd and 3rd in the senior and junior categories at the Isle of Man TT. Calcott is taken over by the Singer Motor Co.

1927 W.J. Green begins making 'York' motorcycles for export. Speedway is introduced in Britain for the first time. Rover halts production of motorcycles to concentrate on making cars. The Hazlewood Co. closes after fifty-one years of manufacturing in the city. W. Handley gains a double victory at the Isle of Man TT in the lightweight and 175cc classes.

1928 In July, Stanley Glanfield embarks on a round-the-world journey on his Rudge motorcycle. Coventry Bees Speedway team is formed at the Foleshill Stadium. Wal Phillips wins the 350cc class race at Brookland's on a Grindlay-Peerless.

1929 German-built Zundapp machines are rebadged and sold under the 'Newmount' name at Warwick Row. 150,000 motorcycles are produced in British factories.

1930 Coventry-based Rudge gain a treble victory at the Junior TT with riders Tyrell-Smith, Nott and Walker, and also wins both the senior and Junior Manufacturers' Team Awards. The Road Traffic Act introduced in December, raising the minimum age of the motorcyclist from 14 to 16 and specifying the need for compulsory insurance. Humber ceases motorcycle production to concentrate on cars.

1931 Triumph releases their budget 'Gloria' machine and Coventry Bicycles Ltd introduce the 'Three Spires' motorcycle. G.W. Walker wins the Isle of Man TT lightweight race on a Rudge. The first edition of the Highway Code is issued.

1932 W.L. Handley and H.G. Tyrell-Smith finish 1st and 2nd respectively in both the Junior and Lightweight class races at the Isle of Man TT, with Handley gaining the fastest lap in the second of 74.08mph in 30.34 minutes.

1933 Rex-Acme ceases all production of motorcycles at their Earlsdon Works. Humber also stops production and concentrates on cars. The co-founder of Triumph, Mauritz Johann Schulte, dies at his home in Marlow, Buckinghamshire aged 76.

1934 J.H. Simpson, G.E. Nott and G.W. Walker gain the treble in the lightweight category race at the Isle of Man TT. Walter Payne, formerly of Payne & Bates Ltd, dies at Coventry aged 71.

1935 Frank Tippen & Sons are established in Coventry. Reflective 'cat's eyes', invented by Percy Shaw, are introduced on British roads.

1936 Both Grindlay-Peerless and Coventry Victor end the manufacture of motorcycles and instead concentrate on general engineering. The future of Triumph motorcycles is secured after Ariel's Jack Sangster takes over the manufacturing rights – production remains in Coventry. Edward Turner is moved over from Ariel and appointed Chief Designer and Managing Director.

1937 Established sidecar manufacturers Mills-Fulford finally close their doors. Triumph

An early image of a Speedway rider Fred Martin practising at Coventry's Brandon Stadium. (John Raven)

The Rudge-Whitworth 250cc model. The company produced motorcycles in Coventry until 1940. (Coventry Transport Museum)

Edward Turners groundbreaking Speed Twin of 1937. (Coventry Transport Museum)

Part of the remaining Triumph Works taken from Pool Meadow in the 1950s. (Coventry Transport Museum)

unveils their 500cc Speed Twin at the Motorcycle Show. Sir Alfred Herbert donates £100,000 to the city of Coventry to build a museum and art gallery. Arthur Barnett of Francis-Barnett dies, and is succeeded by his son Eric.

1938 Coventry Victor ends the production of sidecars. Sunbeam is sold to AJS and Matchless, establishing Associated Motor Cycles Ltd (AMC). BSA launches the famous 'Gold Star' model. Rudge fail to gain any podium finishes at the Isle of Man TT with two retirements.

1939 BSA, Norton, Triumph and others asked to produce motorcycles for the war effort. Coventry Bicycles Ltd creates the 'Petro-Cycle'.

1940 Triumph's Dale Street Works are devastated by German bombs on 14 November. They quickly move to vacant works at Warwick. The war also puts an end to local manufacturers Montgomery and Rudge.

1941 Alfred Robert Grindlay, formerly of specialist motorcycle makers Grindlay-Peerless, is appointed Mayor of Coventry. Percy Riley of the Riley Motor Co. dies aged 58.

1942 Triumph move to new works at a greenfield site at Allesley, Coventry.

1943 AMC sell Sunbeam to BSA.

1944 Motorcycle use declines to an all-time low with just 124,000 taxed for road use. William Riley, founder of the Riley Motor Co., dies at the age of 93. The Antelope Motorcycle Club is formed in Coventry.

Members of Coventry's Antelope Club, established in 1944. (Antelope Club)

1945 The conclusion of the Second World War. Although the country was heavily bombed, some British motorcycle firms excelled. Triumph alone produced 49,700 motorcycles for military duty.

1946 T.G. John, founder of the Alvis Motor Co. and creator of the 'Stafford' auto-scooter, dies aged 66. Italian scooter makers Vespa and Lambretta enter the market.

1947 AMC acquire Francis-Barnett, maintaining their production in Coventry.

1948 Frank Tippen starts the production of the Tippen 'Invalid Chair' at Shakespeare Street. R.H. Pike finishes 2nd on a Rudge in the lightweight class race at the Isle of Man TT. Japanese firm Honda begin making motorcycles. Wartime petrol rationing ends.

1949 Rudge rider R.H. Pike misses out again in the lightweight section of the Isle of Man TT, this time winning a bronze medal. Kawasaki begins making motorcycles in Japan.

1950 The first 'Power-Pak' machine is manufactured in Coventry, while Coventry Eagle ceases the production of motorcycles after fifty-two years.

1951 Triumph is sold to the BSA Group. In the same year, Triumph founder Siegfried Bettmann dies at his home in Coventry.

1952 An A.J.S.-Triumph machine is entered into a lightweight race at the Isle of Man TT, but finishes in a disappointed 18th place. First Suzuki motorcycles produced in Japan.

1953 Marlon Brando stars in the film *The Wild One*, supported by a Triumph motorcycle.

1954 Japanese firm Yamaha established as motorcycle manufacturers.

1955 The company of Smith & Molesworth, established in 1890 and once makers of the 'Alert' motorcycle, finally cease trading in Coventry.

Coventry Eagle began making economical auto-cycles from 1940. (Coventry Transport Museum)

The ever-graceful Muriel Hind seated on her Singer motorcyclette. (Coventry Transport Museum)

1956 Jack Sangster becomes Chairman of the BSA Group. The production of Power-Pak and Tippen machines ends. Pioneering female motorcyclist Muriel Hind dies at her Coventry home aged 74.

1957 British factories' ability to compete in Grand Prix motorcycle races is threatened by rising costs and the introduction of two-stroke engines.

1958 Another ETY-Triumph sidecar racer enters the Isle of Man TT, but fails to improve on the previous year's position, with a 9th place. Victor Riley of the Riley Motor Co. dies at the age of 82.

1959 Eric Cheney combines a Norton frame with a Triumph twin-engine and produces the first Triton motorcycle in England. Triumph wins the World Speed Record at Bonneville, America, with a two-way speed of 139.82mph, commemorating the event by launching one of the most famous motorcycle models of all time, the Bonneville. The Coventry Eagle Co. ends all business activities after almost seventy years of trading.

1960 Learner motorcyclists are restricted to 250cc machines and under. Jack Sangster retires as Chairman of the BSA Group despite record profits of £3,500,000. 1,796,000 motorcycles taxed for road use in Britain – an all-time high.

1961 Cecil Riley of the Riley Motor Co. dies at the age of 66. MOT test are introduced in Britain.

1962 American Bill Johnson pilots a Triumph Bonneville-powered streamliner to a new World Speed Record of 224.57mph. The Coventry Motor Mart, motorcycle agents since 1919, cease trading.

1963 Steve McQueen stars in *The Great Escape*, featuring a Triumph motorcycle.

1964 AMC-owned Francis-Barnett ends all production of motorcycles in Coventry, and move production to Birmingham. Edward Turner retires as Managing Director of Triumph.

1965 After further development, a third Triumph-Norton enters the senior Isle of Man TT and finishes in 15th place. Excelsior, founded as Cycle Manufacturers in Coventry in 1874, end the production of motorcycles at their factory in Birmingham.

Rudge-Whitworth's Rudge-Multi model was initially released in 1911. (Coventry Transport Museum)

1966 Frank Tippen & Sons produce the 'Delta' to rival the AC Invacar. Bob Leppen records a two-way average speed of 245.6mph in America on a Triumph Bonneville-powered streamliner. AMC assets bought by Manganese Bronze Holdings.

1967 AMC becomes Norton-Villiers.

1968 Francis-Barnett ends all production at Birmingham.

1969 *Easy Rider* is released at cinemas across Britain, bringing the 'Chopper' style motorcycle to a British audience.

1970 The Singer name, first used in Coventry on cycles in 1874, is dropped after being taken over by Chrysler.

1971 BSA Group announces a loss of £8.5m. The minimum age of motorcyclist is increased to 17.

1972 BSA Group records a further loss of £3.3m. Coventry Museum's collection of motorcycles is thirty-five strong.

1973 Crash helmets are made compulsory, leading to the formation of the Motorcycle Action Group. Former Ariel, BSA and Triumph Chief Edward Turner dies at the age of 72. BSA Group sold to Norton-Villiers to form a new company, Norton-Villiers-Triumph Ltd (NVT) in July. Plans to move Triumph production to the BSA factory at Small Heath, Birmingham creates a workers sit-in lasting almost two years. Ted Simon begins a round-the-world journey on a Triumph 500cc.

1974 Robert Pirsig's book *Zen and the Art of Motorcycle Maintenance* first published.

1975 Triumph workers dispute ends in a workers' co-operative building the Bonneville and targeting the American market. Front numberplates are no longer required for motorcycles.

1976 Les Williams begins to produce replicas of the 'Slippery Sam', a Triumph Trident winner of five Production Tourist Trophies in the UK.

1977 Triumph launches the limited edition 1977 'Jubilee' Bonneville. Mopeds are restricted to 30mph. Barry Sheene becomes the last Briton to be 500cc Grand Prix World Champion.

The Francis-Barnett Plover, first introduced in 1929. (Coventry Transport Museum)

Above: The Triumph Bonneville took its name through Triumph's record-breaking successes at the Bonneville Salt Flats in America. (Coventry Transport Museum)

Right: The Coventry Victor Co. traded up to 1990. (Coventry Transport Museum)

1978 Experimental 60mph and 70mph speed limits become permanent.

1979 The cult film *Quadrophenia* is released to the British public.

1980 The Museum of British Road Transport is established in Coventry. At this point the motorcycle collection consists of about sixty machines.

1981 Parliament passes the 1981 Transport Act into law, paving the way for new regulations for learner riders.

1982 New riders are required to take two separate tests.

1983 Triumph finally ends the production of motorcycles at their Meriden Plant after eighty-one years of manufacturing. Learner riders are limited to motorcycles no larger than 125cc.

1984 Triumphs Meriden factory is sold and pulled down by developers. A new housing estate is soon built in its place.

1985 Businessman John Bloor revives the Triumph name and establishes Triumph Motorcycles Ltd.

1986 Direction indicator lamps are required for all new motorcycles.

1987 The first national Casualty Reduction Targets laid down by government sees motorcycle injuries reduced by more than half.

1988 Triumph begins to build new works at Hinckley, Leicestershire. Captain Donald M.K. Marendaz, the creator of the Marseal motorcycle, dies at his Lincolnshire home aged 91.

1989 The examiner now follows riders taking their motorcycle test.

1990 Seven years after closing down, Triumph begins production at their new Hinckley factory. Compulsory Basic Training (CBT) is introduced for new riders. Learner riders are prohibited from carrying passengers. Coventry Victor cease to trade.

1991 The famous Coventry landmark, the Rudge-Whitworth factory building is demolished to make way for a leisure complex.

1992 Triumph Tiger becomes the first road bike to be allowed to use a plastic petrol tank in Britain.

1993 Norton finally ceases production of motorcycles.

1994 Sales of new motorcycles start to rise after reaching all-time low of 47,000 in 1993.

1995 Motorcycle use reaches lowest level since the Second World War, as just 594,000 are taxed for British roads.

1996 Triumph celebrates their 40,000th motorcycle built at Hinckley. The Theory Test is introduced for new riders and under 21's are restricted to riding small engine motorcycles for two years after passing their test.

1997 The Museum of British Road Transport stages a special exhibition on 'Sports' motorcycles.

1998 The government invites experts from the motorcycling community to join an Advisory Group for the future of British motorcycling.

1999 Triumph extends their works at Hinckley to cope with increasing demand.

2000 Motorcycle sales in the UK exceeded 170,000 for the first time since 1983.

2001 Ted Simon embarks on his second journey around the world on a motorcycle at the age of 69.

2002 Major gathering of Triumphs in Coventry to celebrate the centenary of the marque (1902). Triumph Works at Hinckley are devastated by fire in March, closing the factory for five months. By September a new factory has been

The Rudge-Whitworth factory shortly before demolition in 1991. (Coventry Transport Museum)

Coventry Transport Museums new motorcycle gallery, opened in April 2006. (Coventry Transport Museum)

A rare Coventry-built Revere motorcycle of 1921, one of many supplied by the British Motorcycle Charitable Trust to Coventry Transport Museum. (Coventry Transport Museum)

erected in its place and production resumed with the launch of the Daytona 600 model.

2003 Hazard Perception testing is introduced for all new riders and drivers to show they are aware of dangerous situations on the road.

2004 The government estimates the number of motorcycles on the road in Great Britain is greater than 1.5 million.

2005 Triumph motorcycles global sales up by 29 per cent on 2004 with sales up by 40 per cent in North America and 34 per cent in Japan. The government publishes its first national strategy for motorcycling. The Institute of Highways Incorporated Engineers publishes guidelines for improving motorcycle safety through engineering better roads.

2006 A new motorcycle gallery is unveiled at Coventry Transport Museum consisting of seventy machines, fifty of which were Coventry-built from 1905 to 2006. Triumph Motorcycles' sales to America exceed 10,000 units for the first time since the company returned to America in 1995. The company aims to break its 1967 record of 28,500 units within the next five years.

2007 The Motor Cycle Industry Association relocates from their Eaton Road address but remains in Coventry, moving to Rye Hill, Allesley.

2008 The British Motorcycle Charitable Trust continues to supply Coventry Transport Museum with rare Coventry-manufactured motorcycles – a 1921 Revere and a 1972 Triumph Bandit.

APPENDIX 5

MANUFACTURING DATES

Coventry Motorcycle Manufacturers & Marques	*Year of Manufacture*
Accles	1896–1898
Acme	1902–1920
A.E.C.	1914–1924
A.E.L.	1919–1924
Alert	1903–1912
Allard	1898–1902
Alpha	1907–1908
A.R.C.	1911–1913
Arno	1906–1915
Atlas	1913–1920
Aurora	1902–1905
Ayton-Riley	1907–
Banholzer, Albert	1942
Beeston	1896–1901
British Challenge	1919–1920
Caesar	1922–1923
Calcott	1905–1915
Centaur	1901–1915
Challenge	1911–1913
Clarendon	1901–1911
C.M.M.	1918–1921
Condor	1907–1924
Coronet	1903–1906
Coventry	1910–1911
Coventry Acme	1920–1922
Coventry B&D	1923–1926
Coventry B&S	1923–
Coventry Challenge	1903–1922
Coventry Crest	1905–1907
Coventry Eagle	1898–1950
Coventry Ensign	1919–1923
Coventry Mascot	1922–1924
Coventry Motette	1897–1903
Coventry Premier	1914–
Coventry Regent	1920–1921
Coventry Star	1919–1921
Coventry Victor	1919–1939
Croft-Anzani	1923–1926
Coventry Motorcycle Manufacturers & Marques	*Year of Manufacture*
Croft-Cameron	1923–1926
Cromwell	1907–
Dart	1923–1924
Davison	1902–1907
D.A.W.	1902–1905
Dingley	1910–1915
Dux	1904–1906
Edwardson	1901
Excelsior	1896–1919
Francis-Barnett	1919–1964
Gamage	1919–1923
Globe	1901–1911
Gloria	1931–1933
Godiva	1900–1901
Gorton	1901–
Grindlay-Peerless	1923–1939
G.S.D.	1921–1923
Hamilton	1901–1907
Hazlewoods	1911–1927
Hillman	1902–
Hobart	1901–1923
Hobart-Acme	1923–1924
H&R	1923–
Hubbard	1904–1905
Humber	1896–1933
Invicta	1912–1926
Johnson-Tyler	1924–1927
Jones, G.	1911–1913
Jones, W.	1924–1927

Coventry Motorcycle Manufacturers & Marques	Year of Manufacture
Kenilworth	1919–1924
Kingsway	1920–1922

Coventry Motorcycle Manufacturers & Marques	*Year of Manufacture*
Lancer	1904–1905
Lawson	1880 & 1900–1901
Lea-Francis	1911–1924
Mars	1922–1926
Marseal	1920–1921
Maxim	1911–1913
McKechnie	1921–1922
McKenzie	1921–1928
Mead	1911–1916
Meri	1911–1913
Midland Motor Cylinder	1926–1927
Millford	1903–1904 & 1933–37
M.M.C.	1897–1904
Mohawk	1912–1925
Monopole	1902–1924
Montgomery	1911–1940
Morton-Adam	1923–1925
Mountaineer	1902–1904
M.S.C.	1906–
New England	1924
New Era	1920–1922
Newmount	1929–1933
New Star	1919–1921
Noble-Precision	1911–1912
Norton	1904–1905
Omega	1919–1927
Omegette	1921–
Osborn	1901–
Pennington	1895–1899
Pennington-Sturmey	1896–
Perks & Birch	1899–1901
Phelon-Humber	1901–1905
Powerful	1903–1906
Power-Pak	1950–1956
P&P	1922–1930
Premier	1908–1920
Progress	1897–1908
Quadrant	1907–1911
Raglan	1902–1903
R&H	1922–1925
Red Arno	1914–1915
Regent	1919–1920

Coventry Motorcycle Manufacturers & Marques	*Year of Manufacture*
Remington	1919–1920
Revere	1915–1922
Rex	1901–1922
Rex-Acme	1922–1933
Rex-Jap	1911–1914
Ridley	1948
Riley	1899–1906 & 1933–1939
Roulette	1911–1914
Rover	1898–1927
Royal Eagle	1901–1910
Rudge	1910–1940
Saxel	1923–1927
Saxessories	1923–
Service	1911–1913
Singer	1900–1921
Spark	1922–1923
Sparkbrook	1912–1926
Stafford	1919–1921
Stan	1919–1921
Stanley	1902–
Star	1919–1921
Starley	1903–
Swift	1898–1915
Three Spires	1931–1932
Tippen	1948–1956
Townend	1901–1904
Triumph	1902–1940 & 1942–1982
Vernon	1919/20–
W.D.	1911–1913
Wee McGregor	1922–1925
Werner	1898–1901
Wheatcroft	1924–
White Heather	*c.* 1915–1925
Whitehouse	1919–1920
White & Poppe	1902–1922
Whitley	1902–1910
Wigan-Barlow	1921–1923
Williamson	1911–1920
Willis	1907–1909
Windrush	1910–1912
York	1927–1930

INDEX

Other titles published by The History Press

Coventry's Bicycle Heritage

DAMIEN KIMBERLEY

Richly illustrated with over 100 outstanding images from Coventry History Centre, many previously unpublished, this is the first book of its kind to cover the history of Coventry bicycle manufacture and the people who built them. From Dunlop, Hobart, Singer, Premier, Rover and Triumph to other lesser-known local companies, their legacies are still enjoyed by cyclists and local historians today.

978 0 7524 5449 8

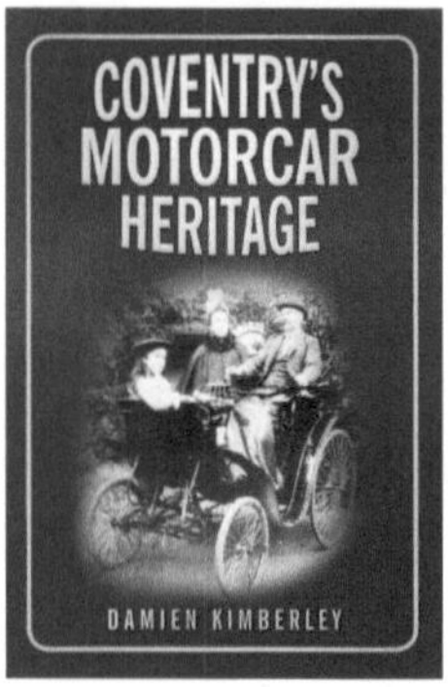

Coventry's Motorcar Heritage

DAMIEN KIMBERLEY

Coventry, home of the cycle industry, was also to become the birthplace of the motor industry when the Daimler Company became the first in Britain to mass produce cars in the late 1890s. Spearheaded by H.J. Lawson, Coventry soon became a hub of motoring activity. This outstanding volume is illustrated with over 150 archive photographs and ephemera, much of which is held at Coventry Transport Museum. This book is a valuable record of the motor companies and their machines, as well as the individuals who both founded and worked for these manufacturers.

978 0 7524 5448 1

Coventry Transport 1884–1940

ROGER BAILEY

When Coventry lost ownership of its local transport system in 1974, it came as a great blow to the many who had worked hard to create such an extensive network of buses, and earlier, trams. Roger Bailey leads us on a detailed and nostalgic pictorial journey through this evolving system, from the long-gone horse-drawn buses of the late 1800s, to the more recognisable diesel buses of the 1930s, via the electric trams which survived the First World War.

978 0 7524 3776 7

British Forces Motorcycles 1925–45

CHRIS ORCHARD & STEVE MADDEN

After centuries of use by the Army for patrols and communications, the trusty horse was finally supplanted by the new-fangled motorcycle. This process of mechanisation gathered pace during the inter-war years and by the outbreak of the Second World War the motorcycle had become an important part of the military inventory. First published in 1995, this edition is fully revised and updated and includes three new chapters, covering standard parts, bike markings and paint schemes. It is the definitive guide to motorcycles used by the British armed forces between 1925 and 1945.

978 0 7509 4451 9

Visit our website and discover thousands of other History Press books.

www.thehistorypress.co.uk